GRIEF BEYOND MEASURE
MEASURE
...BUT NOT BEYOND
GRACE

GRIEF BEYOND MEASURE ...BUT NOT BEYOND GRACE

Help for the Hurting Heart

By
Frank R. Shivers

LIGHTNING SOURCE
1246 Heil Quaker Blvd.
La Vergne, TN

Unless otherwise noted, Scripture quotations are
from
The Holy Bible *King James Version*

Library of Congress Cataloging-in-Publication Data

Shivers, Frank R., 1949-
Spurs to Soul Winning / Frank Shivers
ISBN 978-1-878127-20-4

Library of Congress Control Number:
2013910928

Cover design by
Tim King of Click Graphics, Inc.

For Information:
Frank Shivers Evangelistic Association
P. O. Box 9991
Columbia, South Carolina 29290
www.frankshivers.com

"He will cover you with His feathers; you will take refuge under His wings. His faithfulness will be a protective shield."—Psalm 91:4 HCSB.

Under His wings I am safely abiding,
Though the night deepens and tempests are wild,
Still I can trust Him; I know He will keep me,
He has redeemed me, and I am His child.

Under His wings, what a refuge in sorrow!
How the heart yearningly turns to His rest!
Often when earth has no balm for my healing,
There I find comfort, and there I am blessed.

Under His wings, oh, what precious enjoyment!
There will I hide till life's trials are o'er;
Sheltered, protected, no evil can harm me,
Resting in Jesus, I'm safe evermore.

Under His wings, under His wings,
Who from His love can sever?
Under His wings my soul shall abide,
Safely abide forever.[1]

—William O. Cushing

"Grace be to you and peace from God our Father, and from the Lord Jesus Christ.

"Blessed be God, even the Father of our Lord Jesus Christ, the Father of mercies, and the God of all comfort;

"Who comforteth us in all our tribulation, that we may be able to comfort them which are in any trouble, by the comfort wherewith we ourselves are comforted of God.

"For as the sufferings of Christ abound in us, so our consolation also aboundeth by Christ."
—2 Corinthians 1:2–5.

Presented to

_____

In loving memory of

_____

By

_____

Date

_____

"He heals the brokenhearted and bandages their
wounds."
—Psalm 147:3 NLT.

Only "good-night," beloved—not "farewell!"
A little while, and all His saints shall dwell
In hallowed union, indivisible—
Good-night!
Until we meet again before His throne
Clothed in the spotless robe He gives his own,
Until we know even as we are known—
Good-night![2]

O Lord God, Holy lover of my soul, when Thou shalt come into my heart, all my inward parts shall rejoice. Thou art my glory and the joy of my heart. Thou art my hope and my refuge in the day of my trouble.

But because I am still weak in love and imperfect in virtue, I need to be strengthened and comforted by Thee; therefore, visit Thou me often and instruct me with Thy holy ways of discipline.

Deliver me from evil passions, and cleanse my heart from all inordinate affections, that, being healed and altogether cleansed within, I may be made ready to love, strong to suffer, steadfast to endure.[3]

—Thomas à Kempis

Dedication

This book is dedicated to you who are presently in the valley of devastating pain due to the death of a loved one.

God seems silent and aloof.

Prayers seem unheard.

Exhaustion, emptiness, and loneliness plague.

The "why" question goes unanswered.

The dark night of sorrow seems unending.

Life has lost its luster and sweet fragrance.

Nevertheless, you faithfully look to God, trusting His promises to provide comfort and strength to endure and press on.

You keep praying and waiting.

Because of this, you will not be disappointed; He will turn your mourning into dancing, replacing the garment of grief with that of joy.

Contents

Preface

This is a book for Christian people who are experiencing the agonizing and horrendous emotion of sorrow and grief upon the death of a loved one. Though my walk with grief is similar to what you now experience, it is different due to variables and human make-up. No two people grieve alike. It is within the lenses of the "similar" perspective that *Grief Beyond Measure...but Not Beyond Grace* is written, with hopes it may contribute to your comfort, hope and peace.

The key in reading each entry is to do so prayerfully without hurry so as to soak in its uplifting and healing message. It is my prayer that the God of all comfort will back the dump truck of Heaven up to your hurting heart, dumping tons of love and grace.

1 What Death Means to the Christian

Death—the last sleep? No, the final awakening.[4] —Walter Scott.

God marks across some of our days, "Will explain later."[5]—Vance Havner

"Thou shalt come to thy grave in a full age." "Ah!" says one, "that is not true. Good people do not live longer than others. The most pious man may die in the prime of his youth." But look at my text [Job 5:26]. It does not say thou shalt come to thy grave in old age—but in a "full age." Well, who knows what a "full age" is? A "full age" is whenever God likes to take his children home....There are two mercies to a Christian. The first is that he will never die too soon; and the second, that he will never die too late.[6]—C. H. Spurgeon

Paul wrote Timothy saying, "For I am now ready to be offered, and the time of my departure is at hand" (2 Timothy 4:6). The word "departure" [*analusis*] is a nautical term used to describe a ship lifting anchor and setting sail, an army breaking camp to move out, and a person being freed from his chains. This is what death is to the Christian. It's pulling up anchor and setting sail; it's breaking camp; it's being freed from the cares and trials of this life to go Home.[7]

1

Your loved one in Christ Jesus has done just that. He or she has weighed anchor from this world and set sail for sweet Beulah Land where a grand welcoming party of friends, family and God awaited.

Paul further states about death, 'To be absent from the body is to be present with the Lord' (2 Corinthians 5:8). Death to the Christian is but to enter into the arms of Christ Jesus!

I read a story about a boy whose work required walking home late at night through a cemetery. This was feared each night until he realized that just beyond the cemetery and the graves was home where his father was watching and waiting. There is no need to fear the cemetery or the casket, for just beyond them is Home where the Father is watching and waiting. He will make certain the safe passage of all His children, including your loved one.

Further, Paul declares,

"But I would not have you to be ignorant, brethren, concerning them which are asleep, that ye sorrow not, even as others which have no hope.

"For if we believe that Jesus died and rose again, even so them also which sleep in Jesus will God bring with him.

"For this we say unto you by the word of the Lord, that we which are alive and remain unto the coming of the Lord shall not prevent them which are asleep.

"For the Lord himself shall descend from heaven with a shout, with the voice of the archangel, and with the trump of God: and the dead in Christ shall rise first:

2

"Then we which are alive and remain shall be caught up together with them in the clouds, to meet the Lord in the air: and so shall we ever be with the Lord.

"Wherefore comfort one another with these words." —1 Thessalonians 4:13–18.

W. A. Criswell comments on the passage:

"What of these who have been buried away?" So, he [Paul] writes, "I would not have you without knowledge, my brethren, concerning them which are"—and he uses a word that is distinctly Christian. They used to call it a graveyard, but when the Gospel of the Son of God began to be preached, the Christian people began to use the Greek word *koimeterion*, a sleeping place....The Christians never burned their dead, but they carefully laid them away. And they called the place where they laid their beloved dead a *koimeterion*, a sleeping place. We have it in our language a "cemetery." It's the same Greek word, except we pronounce it in English: cemetery, asleep....May I point out to you he refers to us that we "sleep in Jesus?" He says that Jesus died—died. Jesus died. He died the death of the damned. Jesus died for the unjust. He tasted death for every man. Jesus died....We don't die. We fall asleep."[8]

Your loved one simply has fallen asleep to awaken in God's presence in Heaven.

In the sermon "Go Down, Death," Peter Marshall shared an illustration contrasting death to sleep.

"In a home of which I know, a little boy—the only son—was ill with an incurable disease. Month after month the mother had tenderly nursed him, read to him, and played with him, hoping to keep him from realizing the dreadful finality of the doctor's diagnosis.

"But as the weeks went on and he grew no better, the little fellow gradually began to understand that he would never be like the other boys he saw playing outside his window; and, small as he was, he began to understand the meaning of the term death. And he, too, knew that he was to die.

"One day his mother had been reading to him the stirring tales of King Arthur and his Knights of the Round Table—of Lancelot and Guinevere and Elaine, the lily maid of Astolat, and of that last glorious battle in which so many fair knights met their death. As she closed the book, the boy sat silent for an instant as though deeply stirred with the trumpet call of the old English tale and then asked the question that had been weighing on his childish heart: 'Mother, what is it like to die? Mother, does it hurt?'

"Quick tears sprang to her eyes, and she fled to the kitchen supposedly to tend to something on the stove. She knew it was a question with deep significance. She knew it must be answered satisfactorily. So she leaned for an instant against the kitchen cabinet, her knuckles pressed white against the smooth surface, and breathed a hurried prayer that the Lord would keep her from breaking down before the boy and would tell her how to answer him. And the Lord did tell her. Immediately she knew how to explain it to him.

"'Kenneth,' she said as she returned to the next room, 'you remember when you were a tiny boy how you used to play so hard all day that when night came you would be too tired even to undress and you would tumble into mother's bed and fall asleep? That was not your bed...it was not where you belonged. And you stayed there only a little while. In the morning, much to your surprise, you would wake up and find yourself in your own bed in your own room. You were there because someone had loved you and taken care of you. Your father had come—with big strong arms—and carried you away. Kenneth, death is just like that. We just wake up some morning to find ourselves in the other room—our own room where we belong—because the Lord Jesus loved us.'

"The lad's shining, trusting face looking up into hers told her that the point had gone home and that there would be no more fear...only love and trust in his little heart as he went to meet the Father in Heaven."[9]

Helen Keller declared, "Death is no more than passing from one room into another. But there's a difference for me, you know, because in that other room I shall be able to see."[10]

Martin Luther King said, "Death is not a blind alley that leads the human race into a state of nothingness, but an open door which leads man into life eternal."[11]

The famed evangelist D. L. Moody stated, "Someday you will read in the papers that D. L. Moody of East Northfield is dead. Don't you believe a word of it! At that moment I shall be more alive than I am now; I shall have gone up higher, that is all, out of this old clay tenement into a house that is immortal—a body that death cannot touch, that sin cannot taint; a body fashioned like unto His glorious body."[12]

Even as this became Moody's experience, it now has become that of your loved one.

"Scripture," states C. H. Spurgeon, "continually uses the term *sleep* to express death. Our Savior did. He said, 'Our friend Lazarus sleeps.'...But Jesus spoke not of the transient sleep of the weary, but of the deep slumber of death....When death is called a sleep, it is not because the soul sleeps—that, we are told by Holy Scripture, rises at once to Heaven. The soul of the saint is found at once before the Throne of God. It is the body which is said to sleep. The soul sleeps not! Absent from the body, it is present with the Lord. It stretches its wings and flies away up to yonder realm of joy! And there, reveling in delight, bathing itself in bliss, it finds a rest from the turmoil of earth infinitely better than any rest in sleep. It is the body, then, that sleeps, and the body only."[13]

"The grave," states Alexander MacLaren, "has a door on its inner side."[14] The Christian enters grave's door on earth's side momentarily only to exodus through its unseen door to Heaven. The only Christian that goes to a cemetery is he who mourns the death of another. "Absent from the body...present with the Lord" (2 Corinthians 5:8).

> The only Christian that goes to a cemetery is he who mourns the death of another. "Absent from the body...present with the Lord."
> —2 Corinthians 5:8.

Billy Graham declared, "The word *decease* literally means 'exodus' or 'going out.' The imagery is that of the children of Israel leaving Egypt and their life of bondage, slavery, and hardship for the Promised Land. So death to the Christian is an exodus from the limitations, the burdens, and the bondage of this life."[15]

2   Grace Beyond Measure

"Because of our faith, Christ has brought us into this place of undeserved privilege where we now stand, and we confidently and joyfully look forward to sharing God's glory.

"We can rejoice, too, when we run into problems and trials, for we know that they help us develop endurance.

"And endurance develops strength of character, and character strengthens our confident hope of salvation.

"And this hope will not lead to disappointment. For we know how dearly God loves us, because he has given us the Holy Spirit to fill our hearts with his love." — Romans 5:2–5 NLT.

I am graven on the palms of His hands. I am never out of His mind. All my knowledge of Him depends on His sustained initiative in knowing me. I know Him, because He first knew me and continues to know me. He knows me as a friend, One who loves me; and there is no moment when His eye is off me or His attention distracted for me, and no moment, therefore, when His care falters. This is momentous knowledge. There is unspeakable comfort—the sort of comfort that energizes, be it said, not enervates—in knowing that God is constantly taking knowledge of me in love and watching over me for my good.[16]—J. I. Packer.

Death of a loved one produces grief beyond measure—a hurt so deep that it appears incurable and inescapable. J. I. Packer comes as close as anyone in its description: "Grief: the experiential, emotional fruit of the bereavement event—a state of desolation and isolation, of alternating apathy and agony, of inner emptiness and exhaustion."[17]

Within you, me, and every man lies no capability to manage the painful process of grief, thus making any such attempt foolish. Wherein then does man's hope in such despair lie? David, the psalmist, asked a similar question; and the Holy Spirit revealed the right answer to him.

"Why am I so depressed? Why this turmoil within me? Put your hope in God, for I will still praise Him, my Savior and my God."—Psalm 43:5 HCSB.

Grief indeed is beyond measure to heal yourself but not beyond God's grace to relieve, granting peace and hope. Grace [charis] is the spiritual favor or blessing of God upon man freely bestowed not only with regard to salvation but manifold issues, including grief.

There is no hell on earth so deep but that God's grace can go deeper still, and no sorrow of heart so deep but that God's grace can go deeper still. Where heartache and despair abound, God's grace abounds more. Out of the fullness of Christ Jesus we have and continue to have 'grace upon grace' (John 1:16). No matter how awesome, grand, or superlative you think God's grace to be, it yet is that much greater.

James underscores my point in saying, "He gives a greater grace" (James 4:6 NASB). Grace is greater than our sin but equally greater than our grief.

He's bigger than all the giants of pain and unbelief;

God is bigger than any mountain that I can or cannot see.

He's bigger than any discouragement, bigger than anything;

My God is bigger than any mountain that I can or cannot see.[18]

The words of Jesus to the Apostle Paul are true for all believers: "My grace is enough for you, for my power is made perfect in weakness" (2 Corinthians 12:9 NET). Paul himself said in 2 Corinthians 3:5, "Our sufficiency is from God" (ESV). God's grace is enough, yea more than enough, to bear you up in the hour of deepest sorrow if but to Him you call.

> God's grace is enough, yea more than enough, to bear you up in the hour of deepest sorrow if but to Him you call.

Are you weary; are you heavy hearted?
Tell it to Jesus; tell it to Jesus.
Are you grieving over joys departed?
Tell it to Jesus alone.

Tell it to Jesus; tell it to Jesus.
He is a Friend that's well known.
You've no other such a friend or brother;
Tell it to Jesus alone.

Do the tears flow down your cheeks unbidden?
Tell it to Jesus; tell it to Jesus.[19]
—Edmund S. Lorenz

"I do not say, Suffer not—Jesus suffered. Faith teaches no stoicism. But suffer like men valiant in battle whose wounds, when they smart the most, are incentives to new courage and earnests of future honor.

I do not say, Weep not—Jesus wept. But sorrow not for the Christian dead. They are safe and blest.

I do not say, Shudder not at the thought of death—Jesus trembled when He took the cup into His hand dropping with bloody sweat. It is human nature to shrink from the grave.

But I can say, Fear not. When death comes, you shall have grace to die."[20] And when death comes to a loved one, you will discover new grace with which to cope.

3 It's Okay to Cry

"You keep track of all my sorrows. You have collected all my tears in your bottle. You have recorded each one in your book." —Psalm 56:8 NLT.

Eugene Peterson offers this insight on weeping:

"Jesus wept. Job wept. David wept. Jeremiah wept. They did it openly. Their weeping became a matter of public record. Their weeping, sanctioned by inclusion in our Holy Scriptures, a continuing and reliable witness that weeping has an honored place in the life of faith."[21]

"I am disappointed that someone, somewhere, many years ago, introduced the ridiculous idea that if you know the Lord, you do not grieve. That...you should not weep. With my whole heart I disagree."[22]—Chuck Swindoll.

"Human sorrow is a natural emotion. Our Lord Himself was 'a man of sorrows, and acquainted with grief' (Isa. 53:3). Many things can cause it. We might mourn out of love, disappointment, loneliness, or physical illness. There is nothing wrong with that kind of mourning. It is a God-given relief valve for the pain and sorrow in this fallen world and promotes the healing process."[23]—John MacArthur.

"Then Job arose, and rent his mantle, and shaved his head, and fell down upon the ground, and worshipped,

"And said, Naked came I out of my mother's womb, and naked shall I return thither: the LORD gave, and the LORD hath taken away; blessed be the name of the LORD." —Job 1:20–21.

What happened to the righteous man Job was sudden, without warning. In an instant his children were dead. With this your present experience may identify. Unexpectedly a loved one was snatched away by death, as with Job, leaving you completely stunned, heartbroken and in almost disbelief that it actually happened. How might you respond? No doubt in a manner similar to that of Job who shaved his head, tore his clothes, and fell to the ground in indescribable grief. Job was hurting deeply and poured that hurt out to God in worship seeking comfort. He didn't mask his sorrow or denounce it by counting it unspiritual but freely expressed it as something healthy and beneficial spiritually, emotionally, and physically.

W. A. Criswell shares biblical insight on weeping:

"Is it right for the Christian to cry? Is it right for the Christian to grieve? Is it right for the Christian to be sad and to weep because of the separation of these who have been taken away from us? The answer is yes. It is right. Christ cried those tears. Paul cried those tears. Simon Peter wept those tears. John wept those tears. The saved through the Bible wept those tears. And we weep them, too. The only thing is this: Paul admonishes us that we're not to cry, we're not to weep, we're 'not to sorrow as those who have no hope' (1 Thessalonians 4:13). Beyond our tears is the triumphant grace of God extended to us in Christ Jesus."[24]

Grief is the real deal. I wholeheartedly agree with Criswell. It is okay to experience and express emotions of sorrow and pain. Grief is like medicine to the soul if channeled through God. The psalmist declares,

"The LORD hears his people when they call to him for help. He rescues them from all their troubles.

"The LORD is close to the brokenhearted; he rescues those whose spirits are crushed"—Psalm 34:17–18 NLT.

Psychiatrists attest that grieving is healthy. It's the normal and necessary reaction to the death of one that is loved.

Recall that when Lazarus died Mary and Jesus wept, and others wailed (John 11:34–35). Referencing this text, John R. Rice declared:

"Why did Jesus weep? He knows that in a few minutes He will call Lazarus out of the grave....Oh, but He weeps for the tears of Mary and Martha and others. He weeps with all the broken hearts in the world. He weeps with every mother who loves her [dead] baby, every husband who stands at the casket of his wife. He weeps with every mother or father who weeps in the night over a prodigal boy or wayward girl....But those tears are for me, too, and for you and all who have trouble and sorrow in this world....He is troubled with our troubles....He enters into every sorrow."[25]

And Jesus said, "Come to the water; stand by My
          side.
I know you are thirsty; you won't be denied.
I felt ev'ry teardrop when in darkness you cried,
And I strove to remind you that for those tears I
          died.[26]

"Christ is sufficient," states Elizabeth Elliot. "We do not need support groups for each and every separate tribulation. The most widely divergent sorrows may all be taken to the foot of the same old rugged cross and find there cleansing, peace, and joy."[27]

"I will not leave you comfortless: I will come to you"—John 14:18.

"When we come to Jesus Christ," stated Billy Graham, "He does not promise to exempt us from trouble or sorrow. Tears will come, but deep inside there will be a joy that is difficult to explain to you. It is a joy from God—produced by the Holy Spirit. In the midst of trials and agony and tears which come to us all, a supernatural power is given out, producing joy."[28]

The psalmist offers encouraging words to all who sorrowfully cry, "Weeping may endure for a night, but joy cometh in the morning" (Psalm 30:5). In this text, weeping is pictured as a stranger who lodges with the believer but for the night. The unwanted stranger causes us to toss and turn in unrest, wet our pillow with tears, become mentally and spiritually strained and drained, miserable and helpless. It but appears the night will never end. But certainly it will—and with morning joy cometh!

Thomas Brooks elucidates upon Psalm 30:5:

"Their mourning shall last but till morning. God will turn their winter's night into a summer's day, their sighing into singing, their grief into gladness, their mourning into music, their bitter into sweet, their wilderness into a paradise. The life of a Christian is filled up with interchanges of sickness and health, weakness and strength, want and wealth, disgrace and honor, crosses and comforts, miseries and mercies, joys and sorrows, mirth and mourning. All honey would harm us; all wormwood would undo us. A composition of both is the best way in the world to keep our souls in a healthy constitution."[29]

> It but appears the night will never end. But certainly it will—and with morning joy cometh!

"Tears are a natural form of release," writes Zig Ziglar, "for the still suppressed feelings of love and gratitude, and also for the reservoir of pain and sorrow we have in our hearts."[30]

4   The Stinger of Death Removed

There are valleys too deep for the anguished to find relief. It seems, at that point, there is no reason to go on. We run out of places to look to find relief. It's then that our minds play tricks on us, making us think that not even God cares. Wrong! Do you remember the line that Corrie ten Boom used to quote? I often call it to mind: "There is no pit so deep but that He is not deeper still." I know; I know. Those who are deeply depressed don't remember that and can't reason with it. They would deny such a statement because they feel a vast distance between them and God, and it's confusing—it's frightening. But the good news is that God is not only there…He cares.[31]—Chuck Swindoll.

Our God is Jehovah of hosts, who can summon unexpected reinforcements at any moment to aid His people. Believe that He is there between you and your difficulty, and what baffles you will flee before Him as clouds before the gale.[32]—F. B. Meyer.

Why death? The prophet Isaiah stated, 'The good man perish, the godly die before their time and no one seems to care or wonder why. No one seems to realize that God is taking them away from the evil days ahead. For the godly who die shall rest in peace' (Isaiah 57:1–2). What a thought! Death is God's grace at work protecting saints who die from future heartache. Friends and relatives who die in the

Lord are a trillion times better off than you and I are, for they are at peace in the presence of God.

A boy highly allergic to bee stings riding in the car with his father became terrified when a bee flew in the window. The father stopped the car, allowing the boy to get out while he caught the bee. Back in the car, the boy both saw the bee and heard it buzzing and cried out with fear once again. The boy's fear was calmed when the father simply opened his hand revealing the bee's stinger. Death makes a lot of fuss and noise but is powerless to harm us, for Jesus Christ bore its stinger upon the Cross.

With Paul, the saint can say confidently,

"In a moment, in the twinkling of an eye, at the last trump: for the trumpet shall sound, and the dead shall be raised incorruptible, and we shall be changed.

"For this corruptible must put on incorruption, and this mortal must put on immortality.

"...then shall be brought to pass the saying that is written, Death is swallowed up in victory

"O death where is thy sting, O grave where is thy victory?"

"Thanks be unto God, which giveth us the victory through our Lord Jesus Christ"—1 Corinthians 15: 52–55, 57.

In the times you are afraid of death, do as David and say, 'At what times I am afraid of death I will trust in God who will insure both mine and loved saved ones safe passage into His presence' (Psalm 56:3).

Vance Havner stated, "You haven't lost anything when you know where it is. Death can hide but not divide."[33] You know where your loved ones are, so you haven't lost them. They merely are separated from you for a short while.

If God removes anything from us, He lovingly will put something else in its place. Suffering is eased, relieved to some degree by counterbalancing advantages. In His own wonderful ways, God lets us know that if the roses of life bear thorns, the thorns of life bear roses.[34]

> You know where your loved ones are, so you haven't lost them. They merely are separated from you for a short while.

Francis Ridley Havergal, the hymn writer, shouldered more than her share of sorrow and pain. In a letter to her mother, she writes, "More pain, dearest mother? May it be more support, more grace, more tenderness from the God of all comfort, more and more? May we not expect the 'mores' always to be in tender proportion to each other?"

The "mores" of which she wrote are always in loving proportion to each other. One of these caring "mores" is sympathy—expressed by friends and the sympathizing Jesus.[35]

Amidst the sorrow, God is faithful to manifest His "mores." Expect them and embrace them when they come.

5   *When a Giant Cedar Falls*

"Then they who trust in Jesus will God raise up and bring with Him." He doesn't forsake His own. He doesn't leave to perish in the soil and the dust and the dirt of the earth the least of His saints. If He arose, we shall rise, too—crucified with the Lord, raised with the Lord, translated to meet the Lord.[36]— W.A. Criswell.

"If the Divine Woodman has felled your choicest tree, it may be to reveal blessings hidden beyond. Some of the trees He displaced will be replaced by new ones; indeed, the same ones planted by the Lord in the world to come. Nothing is lost, no one is lost in the economy of God. I will therefore bow in acceptance of the felling of my trees though inwardly I weep."[37]—Vance Havner.

Unless disagreement or estrangement has prompted it to be otherwise, most look to their life-mate or child or parent as a giant cedar in their life. It is a sad day when the giant, great cedar of the forest falls.

"Howl, fir tree for the cedar has fallen."—Zechariah 11:2.

It is right to be saddened and distraught. The cedar which offered shade in the heat of life's struggles, provided guidance in times of misdirection, granted security in life's storms, instilled confidence

23

in the Bible as God's Word and Jesus Christ as the Son of God, pointed the unsaved to the Savior and His church, biblically instructed children and/or students and/or adults in the things of God, patterned how spouses are to love and treat each other and raise their children and/or how children should honor their parents, manifested a meek and humble spirit exhibiting love and grace to all and splashed out the love of Christ everywhere—how could they not be missed?

Of all trees, the cedar is especially useful after it is fallen. It is most useful when dead, most productive when absent from its place. Resistant is its timber to disease or insect. It is incomparable timber also in that it is almost indestructible by time. Often cedar chests are used to preserve a book or garment, protecting from moths and decay. Cedar transfers its unending sweet aroma into the objects around it.

> Your loved one, though now absent, yet transmits an abiding aroma of love and hope to you to press on—and forever will.

Your loved one, though now absent, yet transmits an abiding aroma of love and hope to you to press on—and forever will. Your loved one, though visibly absent, nonetheless is constantly with you through the treasure of a lifetime of precious memories, influence and ministry shared. Retreat to this treasure often, and gain strength and repose.

"Although it's difficult today to see beyond the sorrow,

May looking back in memory help comfort you tomorrow."[38]

The brokenhearted tearfully ask in the time of the "cedar's" removal, "How can the fir tree stand when the cedar is fallen?" How can those who lose their cedars be strong enough to live life without them? The grieving Christian cannot live on feelings, memories or even explanations (though these may be helpful), but upon the promises of God.

"But I have hope when I think of this:

"The LORD'S love never ends; his mercies never stop.

"They are new every morning; LORD, your loyalty is great.

"I say to myself, 'The LORD is mine, so I hope in him.'

"The LORD is good to those who hope in him, to those who seek him.

"It is good to wait quietly for the LORD to save."—Lamentations 3:21–26 NCV.

The believer's "cleft of the rock" that enables life to go on in the absence of a loved one is the Lord Jesus Christ and His bountiful promises.

"Behold, there is a place by Me, and thou shalt stand upon a rock:

"And it shall come to pass, while My glory passeth by, that I will put thee in a cleft of the rock, and will cover thee with My hand while I pass by."—Exodus 33:21–22.

"I will not leave you comfortless: I will come to you."
"But the Comforter, which is the Holy Ghost, whom the Father will send in my name, he shall teach you all things, and bring all things to your remembrance, whatsoever I have said unto you."—John 14:18, 26.

A major work of the Holy Spirit is to comfort the believer. The word "Comforter" means "one to run to our side and pick us up."[39]

The Holy Spirit is with you twenty-four/seven to console, heal, encourage, and strengthen. Don't grieve or hinder Him by shutting Him out (Ephesians 4:30). Don't deprive yourself of His wondrous consolation.

Hold fast to the truth that God makes no mistakes. A. M. Overton expresses this fact beautifully.

He Maketh No Mistake

My Father's way may twist and turn,
My heart may throb and ache,
But in my soul I'm glad to know,
He maketh no mistake.

My cherished plans may go astray,
My hopes may fade away,
But still I'll trust my Lord to lead,
For He doth know the way.

26

When a Giant Cedar Falls

Tho' night be dark and it may seem
That day will never break,
I'll pin my faith, my all, in Him;
He maketh no mistake.

There's so much now I cannot see;
My eyesight's far too dim,
But come what may, I'll simply trust
And leave it all to Him.

For by and by the mist will lift,
And plain it all He'll make,
Through all the way, tho' dark to me,
He made not one mistake.

6 First Steps in Sorrow

"Grief may be called a life-shaking sorrow over loss. Grief tears life to shreds; it shakes one from top to bottom. It pulls him loose; he comes apart at the seams. Grief is truly nothing less than a life-shattering loss."[40]—Jay Adams.

Author Albert Y. Hsu gives this perspective of sorrow:

Christians sometimes think that we are not supposed to grieve, because our faith and theology provide us with confidence about Heaven and eternal life. But while 1 Thessalonians 4:13 says that we are not to grieve as those who have no hope, we grieve nevertheless. Those without hope grieve one way; those with hope grieve another. Either way, grief is universal and not to be avoided. It is a legitimate response to loss.[41]

Articulate your grief. "In some areas of Christianity," states Ron Dunn, "silence is considered to be the proper response to suffering. But silence only deepens the darkness…suffering has an isolating effect on the sufferer. He sees himself forsaken by God and forgotten by everyone else. To remain silent under the burden of suffering means to become more and more isolated. But the Scriptures do not encourage silence or forbid speaking. If we learn anything from Job and Jeremiah and David, and even Jesus—

who cried out on the cross, "My God, My God! Why have You forsaken Me?"—it is that it is right and essential to express the pain of our souls. Sometimes the suffering can be endured only when the pain can be articulated."[42]

Myths and Facts about Grief[43]

MYTH: The pain will go away faster if you ignore it.

Fact: Trying to ignore your pain or keep it from surfacing will only make it worse in the long run. For real healing, it is necessary to face your grief and actively deal with it.

MYTH: It's important to "be strong" in the face of loss.

Fact: Feeling sad, frightened, or lonely is a normal reaction to loss. Crying doesn't mean you are weak. You don't need to "protect" your family or friends by putting on a brave front. Showing your true feelings can help them and you.

MYTH: If you don't cry, it means you aren't sorry about the loss.

Fact: Crying is a normal response to sadness, but it's not the only one. Those who don't cry may feel the pain just as deeply as others. They may simply have other ways of showing it.

MYTH: Grief should last about a year.

Fact: There is no right or wrong time frame for grieving. How long it takes can differ from person to person.

David's baby was seriously ill, so he fasted and prayed unto God for the child's healing. The child died. Upon hearing the news, David took a bath, put on fresh garments, and went into the house of God and worshiped. Upon returning home, he broke his fast and enjoyed a good meal (2 Samuel 12:20–21).

David's servants were puzzled, failing to understand how he so soon could return to some normalcy of life. David said,

"I fasted and wept while the child was alive, for I said, 'Perhaps the LORD will be gracious to me and let the child live.'

"But why should I fast when he is dead? Can I bring him back again? I will go to him one day, but he cannot return to me."—2 Samuel 12: 22–23.

You need to do what King David did in the hour of deepest grief.

David returned to church.

In addition to the worship of God, it provides support from fellow believers, some of which have walked in similar steps as you now tread.

Phillip Yancy cautions, "Do not attempt healing alone. The real healing of deep connective tissue takes place in community. Where is God when it hurts? Where God's people are. Where misery is, there is the Messiah; and on this earth, the Messiah takes form in the shape of his church. That's what the body of Christ means."[44]

David engaged in prayer.

Sorrow ought to bring us to our knees, for the believer's true source of strength and comfort comes through prayer from the throne of God. Express unto God the anger, pain, sorrow, and doubts you are battling. "Our healing from grief," states Zig Ziglar, "to a very great extent, lies in our daily communication with the Lord."[45]

David got back to work.

"So David gathered all the people together and went to Rabbah, fought against it, and took it."—2 Samuel 12:29.

Those who are sorrowing are to keep on working despite the tears of brokenheartedness. Keep teaching that church class, singing in the choir, soul winning, working with the children/student ministry, preaching, singing despite the tears, and in doing so find comfort and healing. Don't desert the ministry God has called you to perform during your grief, no matter how difficult it is. Keep pressing on in His strength and by His grace.

Michael Card comments in *A Sacred Sorrow:*

"The same stubborn refusal to let go of God that is expressed in his laments empowered David to stubbornly refuse to be destroyed by the grief of innocent death and the despair of knowing it was all a consequence of his sin. The painful realities of death and sin had somehow been dealt with during his time of lament. They had been offered in worthship to the God David was beginning to learn could be trusted. Only by realizing the reality of pain and acknowledging through lament to God our powerlessness and hopelessness can we arrive at such a place of freedom as David inhabited."[46]

David by God's grace accepted the death of his child though he didn't understand it. Doubtful that you presently or ever will understand the death of your loved one, but by God's grace faith must be extended to trust Him by submitting to it as His divine will.

"When parents experience the death of a child [like David]," remarks John MacArthur "one of the first questions they are likely to ask is, 'Why did my child have to die?' Generally the emphasis in asking the question is 'Why did *my* child have to die?'

"...There is no easy answer to that question. The answer begins with the fact that life is marked by difficulty and sorrow. We live in a fallen world. We live in a world flawed by disease and sin. Trouble comes to us as part of our human condition.

"...God is omnipotent. He is also omniscient. As a result, some of His purposes and plans we cannot know this side of eternity. God may have allowed a child to die for reasons that will never be understood—reasons that may involve the lives of the parents, the lives of siblings, the life of the child himself, the lives of others unknown by the parents or child.

> The Holy Scripture is the believer's indispensable source of comfort in the hour of sorrow. Many are the passages within the Bible that speak comfort to the sorrowing heart.

"There is a question even more potent than the question 'Why did my child have to die?' That question is 'What does God desire for me to do in the midst of this tragedy?' The question of 'Why?' has no satisfactory answer. The question of 'What now?' can turn a person from grief to action, from loss to healing, from sorrow to joy, and from feelings of utter devastation to feelings of purpose."[47]

David also rested upon the Bible.

He knew the Scripture well enough that he could say with confidence that though he couldn't bring his child back, he could one day be with his child in Heaven. The Holy Scripture is the believer's indispensable source of comfort in the hour of sorrow. Many are the passages within the Bible that speak comfort to the sorrowing heart (Psalm 23; John 14; Romans 8:37–39; 1 Corinthians 15:51–58; 1 Thessalonians 4:13–18; Revelation 7:9–17; Revelation 21:1–4; and Psalm 90). Scripture will be medicine to your broken heart like none other, granting healing.

Take one step at a time at your own pace, but do what David did, and the peace and comfort of God will rule your heart.

"Pain and suffering and sorrow," states W. A. Criswell, "have a purpose in our lives. They are the means and instruments and ways of God to teach us to be humble and to be compassionate and to love the Lord and lean upon His kind heart—the end of sorrow, the beginning and the end, the end of sorrow."[48]

A grieving widow sought advice from Billy Graham regarding tremendous grief. She shared, "My friends tell me that I should forget the past, but this is not easy when it's all I have." Graham replied:

"When one tries to recapture that which is gone forever, it brings frustration and sometimes depresssion. Jesus said to His troubled disciples, 'Let not your heart be troubled; ye believe in God, believe also in me.' Two things are revealed in these words. First, we each have the power to expel worry and trouble and even sorrow from our minds. Jesus said, 'Let not,' and this signifies that we control trouble and sorrow or at least our attitude toward it. Second, He said, 'Ye believe in God, believe also in me.' To believe in God and His Son, Jesus Christ, means that we believe that Heaven makes no mistakes. Remember this: God never did an unkind thing to His children."[49]

"God is too good to be unkind, too wise to be mistaken"; states C. H. Spurgeon, "and when you cannot trace His hand, you can trust His heart."[50]

J. R. Miller, in the sermon "Afterward You Will Understand," offers excellent insight with regard to the "Why" question about your loved one's death. Miller states, "But all the mysteries in our lives will someday be revealed. They will not always be inexplicable to us. 'What I am doing, you do not understand now; but afterward you will understand' (John 13:7). We do not see now how this or that experience can be well and can do good, but after a time the mystery is explained. It is only afterwards that many of God's providences can be clearly understood. It takes time for the full meaning to be wrought out. We do not know in the days of sorrow what 'shining blessing' will be revealed as the final outcome. We do not see in midwinter the roses that are hidden under the snow which after a while will unfold their beauty.

"There is a distinct promise that the mysteries of life will be made clear sometime. Ofttimes this is realized soon. There are some of life's mysteries, however, which are never made plain in this present world. Life is too short. Godly people die sometimes with perplexities unexplained. But there is another life. We are immortal. We shall live forever after leaving earth. There will be time enough then for the deepest mysteries to be made plain."[51]

7   Heaven Is for Real

"If you knew what God knows about death, you would clap your listless hands."[52]—George MacDonald

Jesus states that Heaven is a place (John 14:2). It is a place just as much as the city in which you reside is a place. If it were not, the Bible would not speak of its streets of pure gold, walls of jasper, foundations of twelve precious stones, gates of pearl, or its inhabitants. To the liberals who claim this description of Heaven is simply figurative language, Jesus responds, "If it were not so, I would have told you." In other words, Jesus is saying, "If Heaven were not like I described it, I would have told you so!"

Believers must remember that besides the little we know about Heaven, there is far more that we do not know. Paul affirms this truth:

"But as it is written, Eye hath not seen, nor ear heard, neither have entered into the heart of man, the things which God hath prepared for them that love him."—1 Corinthians 2:9.

The best description of Heaven fails to touch the hem of its awesome glorious garment. In Heaven there are "many mansions" (John 14:2).

Heaven was designed to accommodate the innumerable multitudes who would enter its domain.

There is no danger of insufficient housing for the ransomed of God. Jesus' use of the term "mansions" (rooms or apartments) indicates distinct, private accommodations for each of His children.[53]

The believer's apartment in Heaven will never need maintenance or replacement, for it is eternally durable.

"To those who doubt the existence of Heaven because, no matter how far we travel in space, we have yet to locate it, consider the following facts. The distance between the electrons and the nucleus of an atom being proportionate to the distance between Pluto and the sun, all matter on this earth is composed of ninety-five percent space—leaving plenty of room for an unseen dimension to coexist with the material world we presently perceive."[54]

> The believer's apartment in Heaven will never need maintenance or replacement, for it is eternally durable.

"Hope sees beyond the cloud," comments R. G. Lee, "beyond the obstacle, beyond the hardship, beyond the weakness, beyond the failure, beyond the difficulty. Hope says to us, 'Never accept the verdict of your defeat, the verdict of your melancholy, the verdict of your sickness, the verdict of your disaster, the verdict of your disappointment.' The psalmist says, 'Thou hast made me to hope.' And Jesus said, 'If it were not so [about there being many mansions in

His Father's house, many of them], I would have told you.'"[55]

Rest assured that your loved one, if a Christian, awaits your arrival in that land the hymn writer describes as "Sweet Beulah Land," "a land that is fairer than day," and "The Sweet By and By."

At what moment do we enter Heaven? Paul pointedly states that to be absent from the body is to be present with the Lord (2 Corinthians 5:8). At the moment that Lazarus died, angels escorted him into the presence of God in Heaven (Luke 16:22). The saint shuts his eyes in death and opens them instantly in Heaven.

The epitaph on the tombstone of Solomon Peas, London, England, expresses this biblical truth.

Beneath these clouds and beneath these trees
Lies the body of Solomon Peas.
This is not Peas; it is only his pod.
Peas has shelled out and gone Home to God.[56]

At age thirty-eight, the writer of the glorious hymn "Rock of Ages," Augustus Toplady, died in London. As death approached, he exclaimed, "It is my dying vow that these great and glorious truths which the Lord in rich mercy has given me to believe and enabled me to preach are now brought into practical and heartfelt experience. They are the very joy and support of my soul. The comfort flowing from them carries me far above the things of time and sin....Had I wings like a dove, I would fly away to the bosom of God and be at rest."

Toplady's last words were, "Oh! What delight! Who can fathom the joys of Heaven! I know it cannot be long now until my Savior will come for me." And then bursting into a flood of tears, he said, "All is light, light, light, light, the brightness of His own glory. Oh, come, Lord Jesus, come. Come quickly!"[57] And he was ushered into the presence of God.

> While I draw this fleeting breath,
> When mine eyes shall close in death,
> When I soar to worlds unknown,
> See Thee on Thy judgment throne,
> Rock of Ages, cleft for me,
> Let me hide myself in Thee.

8 You Will Know Your Loved One in Heaven

Believe me, every heart has its secret sorrows which the world knows not, and often times we call a man cold when he is only sad.[58]—Henry Wadsworth Longfellow

"For now we see through a glass, darkly; but then face to face: now I know in part; but then shall I know even as also I am known"—1 Corinthians 13:12.

In their heavenly (resurrected) bodies, Jesus, Moses, and Elijah were recognized (John 20:16; Matthew 17:1–4). Jesus said that we will see "Abraham, and Isaac, and Jacob, and all the prophets, in the kingdom of God" (Luke 13:28).

I believe part of the comfort Paul refers to for believers in 1 Thessalonians 4:14–18 is knowledge of a reunion day coming in Heaven with loved ones. The saints in Heaven will fellowship not only with their redeemed marriage mates, parents, children, grandparents, and friends, but also with all other redeemed people not known to the believer during life on earth. This includes the prophets, disciples, patriarchs, missionaries, and evangelists.

The narrative already cited regarding the death of David's child teaches that your child on earth will be your child in Heaven; and, thus, your mother will be your mother, your father be your father, and so on. Obviously the role in the relationship will change in Heaven, but the relationship will continue (2 Samuel 12:22–23 NLT).

W. A. Criswell, in *Heaven*, states that one's personality survives in Heaven, that we each will be who we are now but without the baggage of sin and imperfection.[59] Further, Criswell states, "We shall not know less of each other in Heaven; we shall know more. We shall possess our individual names in Heaven. We shall be known as individuals.

> The saints in Heaven will fellowship not only with their redeemed marriage mates, parents, children, grandparents, and friends, but also with all other redeemed people not known to the believer during life on earth.

You will be you; I shall be I; we shall be we. Personality and individuality exist beyond the grave."[60]

Jesus' resurrection body is the prototype for the redeemed of God (1 Cor. 15:20, 48–49; Phil. 3:21; 1 John 3:2). In the resurrection body, He walked, talked, and ate (John 21:1–14). Jesus even dismissed the idea that saints in the afterlife would be "disembodied spirits" (Luke 24:37–39). The saint's spirit immediately at death enters the presence of the Lord; later, at the rapture of the church, it will be reunited with its body, which will be transformed into a glorified body likened to that of Christ (1 Thessalonians 4:16; 1 John 3:2).

Commenting on the resurrection of Christ, Norman Geisler said, "While His resurrection body is more than mortal, it is not less than physical."[61] Geisler continues, "The New Testament is emphatic that Jesus rose in the same body of flesh and bones in which He died."[62] The believer's resurrection body will be the same, enabling recognition.

F. B. Meyer, in a letter to a friend, wrote, "I have just heard to my great surprise that I have but a few days to live. It may be that before this reaches you, I shall have entered the palace. Don't trouble to write. We shall meet in the morning."[63]

F. B. Meyer's words echo the sentiment of all who die in the Lord. A glad reunion day awaits with loved ones "in the morning."

I'll meet you in the morning with a "How do you do?"
And we'll sit down by the river and with rapture old
    acquaintance renew.
You'll know me in the morning by the smile that I
    wear,
When I meet you in the morning in the city that is
    built foursquare.[64]

43

9   Does Jesus Care?

"We are afflicted in every way, but not crushed; perplexed, but not despairing; persecuted, but not forsaken; struck down, but not destroyed." —2 Corinthians 4:8–9.

"There is nothing—no circumstance, no trouble, no testing—that can ever touch me until, first of all, it has gone past God and past Christ right through to me. If it has come that far, it has come with a great purpose, which I may not understand at the moment. But as I refuse to become panicky, as I lift up my eyes to Him and accept it as coming from the throne of God for some great purpose of blessing to my own heart, no sorrow will ever disturb me; no trial will ever disarm me; no circumstance will cause me to fret—for I shall rest in the joy of what my Lord is! That is the rest of victory!"[65]—Alan Redpath

Commenting on Psalm 139:3, C. H. Spurgeon emphasizes the never ceasing presence of God with His children. "Thou compassest my path and my lying down." My path and my pallet, my running and my resting, are alike within the circle of Thine observation. Thou dost surround me even as the air continually surrounds all creatures that live. I am shut up within the wall of Thy being; I am encircled within the bounds of Thy knowledge. Waking or sleeping I am still observed of Thee. I may leave Thy path, but You never leave mine. I may sleep and forget Thee, but Thou dost never slumber nor fall into oblivion concerning Thy creature.

Does Jesus care when my heart is pained
Too deeply for mirth or song,
As the burdens press, and the cares distress,
And the way grows weary and long?

Does Jesus care when my way is dark
With a nameless dread and fear?
As the daylight fades into deep night shades,
Does He care enough to be near?

Does Jesus care when I've said "good-bye"
To the dearest on earth to me?
And my sad heart aches till it nearly breaks—
Is it aught to Him? Does He see?

Oh, yes, He cares; I know He cares.
His heart is touched with my grief.
When the days are weary, the long nights dreary,
I know my Savior cares.[66]

Death is not a matter of unconcern to God for either the saint who dies or his loved ones who remain. Yes, "His heart is touched with my

> Death is not a matter of unconcern to God for either the saint who dies or his loved ones who remain.

grief." The psalmist declared,

"Precious in the sight of the LORD is the death of his saints."—Psalms 116:15.

David calls the death of a saint precious. Certainly this strange epithet of death is not easy for us to grasp when it has snatched our loved one.

In earlier burial instructions, "Precious in the sight of the LORD is the death of his saints" with other verses was to be chanted.[67] The practice may not be a bad custom to reinstitute.

Why is a saint's death precious in the sight of the Lord? Or to make it personal, why is the death of your loved one precious in His sight?

It is precious due to its freeing power from suffering, sorrow, and sickness. Those who die in the Lord sing, "Free at last, free at last—praise God Almighty, I am free at last."

It is precious in that it removes the saint from the present evil on earth and that which is yet to come.

It is precious in that it puts on display the comforting grace of God as a witness to the world of how God sustains His children in the severest trial of sorrow, granting peace and solace.

The death of a saint is precious in the sight of the Lord in that it means he/she is now with Him in Heaven.

It is also precious in the fact that it may be the means of conversion of family and friends.

47

But saying the death of the saints is precious in His sight indicates that the death of the unbeliever is not. Why not?

It is because at death the non-Christian is forever in Hell separated from God and the Christian (Revelation 20:15). This is not God's desire. He longs for every person to be saved and enjoy a relationship with Him and saved loved ones today, tomorrow and forever in Heaven! Heaven is the eternal dwelling place of the redeemed family of God.

The *entrance ticket* into this celestial city is not church membership, baptism, confirmation, right-eousness, or good deeds, but a personal relationship with Jesus Christ through the new birth (John 3:3; Acts 20:21). Jesus, in discussing His ascension to Heaven to make preparation for the saints, was asked by Thomas to clarify the way to this celestial abode (John 14:5). Jesus answered Thomas,

"I am the way, the truth, and the life: no man cometh unto the Father, but by me."—John 14:6.

Jesus is the only *Door* to this celestial city (John 10:9). Guidance for entering this *Door* is provided in Chapter 23 of this book.

John Wesley as he was about to enter the Celestial City said, "The best of all is God is with us."[68] How comforting these words were to his family, friends and followers and to all today who witness the exodus of a loved one from the temporal sphere to the eternal!

10   What Grief Looks Like

Author and theologian C. S. Lewis' wife died of cancer three years after they were married. In *A Grief Observed,* Lewis shares the process of grieving he experienced, from which the excerpt below is taken.

"No one ever told me that grief felt so like fear. I am not afraid, but the sensation is like being afraid. The same fluttering in the stomach, the same restlessness, the yawning. I keep on swallowing. At other times it feels like being mildly drunk, or concussed. There is a sort of invisible blanket between the world and me. I find it hard to take in what anyone says—or perhaps, hard to want to take it in. It is so uninteresting. Yet I want the others to be about me. I dread the moments when the house is empty. If only they would talk to one another and not to me."[69]

"Bereavement becomes a supreme test of the quality of our faith."[70]—J. I. Packer

Knowledge is power in many respects, but not any more so than with regard to the grief process. In knowing its various states [what to expect and when and how to cope with each], the pain and disruption of life will be lessened.

> Knowledge is power in many respects, but not any more so than with regard to the grief process.

Shock (numbness, disbelief), irritability, anxiety, guilt, anger, depression, loneliness and acceptance/ adjustment are emotions grievers may experience. You may be experiencing one or more of these emotions presently. The cycle of emotions tends to teach that such emotions may subside temporarily only to resurface many times during the acute phase of one's loss (the first few years after the death of your loved one). Should you become "stuck" in such emotional responses and unable to break free, seek out professional Christian counseling.

Shock, Numbness and Disbelief

These may occur as result of a loved one's death, especially when it is unexpected. The numbness (appearance of being unaffected by the death) will linger, to dissipate only gradually.

Irritability

The anxiety and stress of a loved one's death may lead to irritability or agitation. This may be ignited by something as mundane as a person chewing flavored gum, crowding your space, and speaking loudly. Or it could be something larger like a family or friend criticizing how you are dealing with grief or the funeral arrangements you have made. You may not always control the arousal of irritability, but you can control its response (step back and take several deep breaths, avoid a knee-jerk reaction by thinking prior to speaking, excuse yourself and walk away).

If you respond to the agitation with harsh words, apologize without delay, for your mental and spiritual health as well as theirs. In instances when others constantly cause irritability, tactfully take steps to reveal that to them (more than likely they don't realize they are doing this). Irritability will lessen as the grieving process progresses.

Anxiety

Upon the death of a loved one, anxiety impacts everyone who is dependent upon another (a wife upon her husband, a child upon a parent, a child worrying about the other parent's dying). Scripture offers comfort to all who suffer anxiety.

"Give all your worries and cares to God, for he cares about you."—1 Peter 5:7 NLT.

Guilt

This plagues the survivor ("If I only hadn't given my son permission to go to that event, the accident that took his life would never have happened"; "If I had driven that night instead of my wife, she would still be alive"; "Why didn't the doctor catch his/her condition sooner?" "If I had done _____, she/he would still be alive." Guilt evolves into the blame game, "second guessing" which is unhealthy. The plain fact is that you must trust God with what has happened and press forward. Jesus relieves guilt upon request by forgiving what prompted it (1 John 1:7–9).

Anger

Anger regarding the cause of the death may surface (drunk driver, a texting motorist, a life guard who wasn't alert, a doctor), or you could be angry with yourself for not having the chance to reconcile after an argument. Sadly, it may even extend to God. God is big enough to handle our anger toward others, ourselves and Himself and help it be diffused. "Your pains," states C. H. Spurgeon, "are sharp. From the pains of Hell Christ has delivered you. Why should a living man complain? As long as you [and your departed loved one] are out of Hell, gratitude may mingle with your groans."[71]

Anger may also be directed toward family members if you perceive them as overstepping their bounds in funeral service planning. In the traumatic early hours of deep sorrow upon the death of a loved one, decision making with regard to the funeral service is not easy, but it is necessary. Inasmuch as possible, the wishes of the deceased and family members should be honored (if such glorify God). The key is to understand the "inasmuch as possible." No matter how much is included (preaching, singing, etc.), one may wish after the service that another song had been sung or something else had been said or another minister had been invited to share, etc. This can lead to becoming bitter toward other family members for the exclusion.

Choke this down. Give it no breath. Give no place to it. Bury it. It is an emotion stirred by Satan endeavoring to create further havoc and heartache for you personally and in the lives of others. Don't allow the separation of a loved one in death to prompt another one in life by bearing the poison of anger or hostility. Anger toward the family or funeral home that continues to resurface following a loved one's death needs therapeutic help from a Christian grief counselor.

"Make allowance for each other's faults, and forgive anyone who offends you. Remember, the Lord forgave you, so you must forgive others."—Colossians 3:13 NLT.

"Finally, all of you should be of one mind. Sympathize with each other. Love each other as brothers and sisters. Be tenderhearted, and keep a humble attitude.

"Don't repay evil for evil. Don't retaliate with insults when people insult you. Instead, pay them back with a blessing. That is what God has called you to do, and he will bless you for it."—1 Peter 3:8–9 NLT.

Depression

"What is depression?" declares Adrian Rogers. "A psychologist has described depression this way: a feeling of helplessness and hopelessness that leads to sadness. I think that's a good definition. A person who is depressed has problems, real or imagined, and he doesn't seem to be able to get a handle on them. There's no help available, and that's compounded by the fact that there doesn't seem to be any help on the horizon. It's helplessness plus hopelessness that leads to this deep despondency, this sadness."[72]

The loss of a loved one fuels depression. This depression is a normal and healthy response to death. In fact, it would be unusual for a person not to experience depression to some degree after a loved one dies.

"In a desert land he found him, in a barren and howling waste. He shielded him and cared for him; he guarded him as the apple of his eye."—Deuteronomy 32:10.

"I waited patiently for the LORD; he inclined to me and heard my cry.

He drew me up from the pit of destruction, out of the miry bog, and set my feet upon a rock, making my steps secure.

He put a new song in my mouth, a song of praise to our God. Many will see and fear, and put their trust in the LORD."—Psalm 40:1–3.

"Why are you cast down, O my soul, and why are you in turmoil within me? Hope in God; for I shall again praise him, my salvation and my God."—Psalm 42:11.

The famous London pastor C. H. Spurgeon testified, "I find myself frequently depressed—perhaps more so than any other person here. And I find no better cure for that depression than to trust in the Lord with all my heart and seek to realize afresh the power of the peace-speaking blood of Jesus and His infinite love in dying upon the cross to put away all my transgressions."[73]

Loneliness

"Turn to me and be gracious…for I am lonely."—Psalm 25:16.

In research for this book, I couldn't put down Vance Havner's *Hope Thou in God* which to some degree chronicles his journey of grief following the death of his wife of thirty-three years, Sara. I scarcely could hold back the tears as I read of his dire loneliness, a recurring theme in the book.

Writing of Sara, he states, "Yes, the communication is cut now for a season, and I can't get through. The heart grows restless, and the wait seems long, but we have all eternity to make up for it." Then Havner exclaims to all who have experienced the death of a loved one, "We have not heard those voices, now stilled, for the last time; nor have we seen those faces finally. What the new face and voice will be like remains to be seen and heard, but our present equipment would not be able to take it if we could."[74]

"God makes a home for the lonely."—Psalm 68:6 NASB.

The prayer of Augustine for all who suffer loneliness:

"God of our life, there are days when the burdens we carry chafe our shoulders and weigh us down; when the road seems dreary and endless, the skies grey and threatening; when our lives have no music in them and our hearts are lonely and our souls have lost their courage. Flood the path with light, run our eyes to where the skies are full of promise, tune our hearts to brave music, give us the sense of comradeship with heroes and saints of every age, and so quicken our spirits that we may be able to encourage the souls of all who journey with us on the road of life, to Your honor and glory."[75]

Acceptance/Adjustment

Don't equate acceptance of a loved one's death as being okay with it. You will never be okay with it. Rather, it means facing the new reality that your loved one is gone physically, never to return. This is not easy, but small steps will turn into big steps in learning to live in a world without your soul mate or child or parent or friend. He/she will be sorely missed. Adjustment to a life without him/her happens in bits and pieces, but it must and will. Guilt may be encountered initially in "moving on," thinking that such is a betrayal of him/her, but this is untrue. Anticipate and prepare for *surprise* recurrences of grief after its initial departure. A smell of fragrance or cologne, an event, a television show, or the resurfacing of a memory all may be triggers to grief. Expect grief to surprise you time and again, which is completely healthy and normal. Develop a recovery plan to use to minimize discomfort and pain when these surprises arise.

You may experience one or more of these emotions or one not listed. Regardless of the emotion, remember to bring it to the Lord for help and healing. There is nothing that you and God cannot handle together.

11 Refuge for the Hurting Heart

There is no mention in the Bible of Jesus ever laughing, but He was often observed weeping.[76]— Henry M. Morris

Vance Havner, on the death of his wife, Sara, said, "How can I ever praise God again after this? We grow bitter when some pitying soul who has never been there recites all the clichés and platitudes. But it works. I thought I could never be happy again making my lonely way bereft of my companion. I do not understand the why of it all. That waits for Heaven. But faith does not wait for explanation to begin praising. Faith does not wait to understand. We have His Word, and if it were not so, He would have told us."[77]

> Death leaves a heartache no one can heal;
> Love leaves a memory no one can steal.
> —An Irish Headstone

Dos and Don'ts During the Grief Process[78]

Dr. Timothy Faulk, Certified Trauma Specialist, states that people who experience grief may often demonstrate changes in behavior. He provides some do-and-don't suggestions that will help reduce the probability of long-term reactions.

*Do*s

•Get enough rest.

•Maintain regular diet.

•Take one thing at a time.

•Follow a familiar routine.

•Talk to supportive people.

•Maintain exercise regimen.

•Spend time with family/friends.

•Expect the experience to upset you.

*Don't*s

•Don't stay away from work.

•Don't withdraw from others.

•Don't look for easy answers.

•Don't increase caffeine intake.

•Don't reduce leisure activities.

•Don't make major life changes.

•Don't take on new major projects.

•Don't have unrealistic expectations.

Solomon tells us in Proverbs 18:10 that God's name is "like a strong tower" that keeps us safe and secure from the enemy (Satan). A tower in biblical days provided protection for people in times of different types of emergencies.

For example, when an enemy was about to attack, they would run into this strong tower and be kept safe. God's name is like that strong tower for us. In times of emergencies (all sorts of trouble or crisis or problems), call on God's name; and He will grant protection.

This tower is so deep that no bomb can undermine it, so thick that no missile can penetrate it, so high that no ladder can scale it or arrow of Hell reach it. The psalmist declares,

"For he will conceal me there when troubles come; he will hide me in his sanctuary. He will place me out of reach on a high rock." —Psalm 27:5.

Run into the strong tower of the name(s) of the Lord in the time of sorrow and find comfort, peace, and serenity.

Jehovah-Jireh:

The Lord who sees your need and, because He sees it, will provide for it (Genesis 22:1–14).

"But my God shall supply all your need according to his riches in glory by Christ Jesus." —Philippians 4:19.

Jehovah-Shalom:

The Lord desires you to know peace amidst life's storms (Judges 6:24; Romans 5:1).

He grants peace.

"For I know the thoughts that I think toward you, saith the LORD, thoughts of peace, and not of evil, to give you an expected end."—Jeremiah 29: 11.

Jehovah-Rohi:

The Lord who shepherds His people.

Shepherds protect their flock by stationing themselves between them and the deadly wolf and makes provision for their every need. Jesus is your Good Shepherd.

"The LORD is my shepherd; I shall not want.

"He maketh me to lie down in green pastures: he leadeth me beside the still waters.

"He restoreth my soul: he leadeth me in the paths of righteousness for his name's sake.

"Yea, though I walk through the valley of the shadow of death, I will fear no evil: for thou art with me; thy rod and thy staff they comfort me."—Psalm 23:1–4.

El-Elyon:

The extremely-exalted, sovereign high God who is in total control.

Nothing can happen in your life without His permission.

"I will cry to God Most High, To God who accomplishes all things for me."—Psalm 57:2 NASB.

J. B. Phillips wrote the book *Your God Is Too Small*, and the title tells the tale. For many (perhaps yourself), their *God Is Too Small.*

Grasp the fact that God is Jehovah-Jireh, Jehovah-Shalom, Jehovah-Rohi, and El-Elyon; and it will change your thinking about what has been, what is, and what will be. In the midst of great pain and sorrow, *run* into the strong tower of God by claiming the promise His names characterize and abide safely in the pavilion of His loving care.

"Too often we sigh," declares Theophilus Stork, "and look within; Jesus sighed and looked without. We sigh and look down; Jesus sighed and looked up. We sigh and look to earth; Jesus sighed and looked to Heaven. We sigh and look to man; Jesus sighed and looked to God!"[79]

Jesus, my heart's dear Refuge, Jesus has died for
    me;
Firm on the Rock of Ages, ever my trust shall be.
Here let me wait with patience, wait till the night is
    o'er;
Wait till I see the morning break on the golden shore.
Safe in the arms of Jesus, safe on His gentle breast,
There by His love o'ershaded, sweetly my soul shall
    rest.[80]

12 The Day of Sorrow Will Pass

God knows just when to withhold from us any visible sign of encouragement and when to grant us such a sign. How good it is that we may trust Him anyway! When all visible evidences that He is remembering us are withheld, that is best; He wants us to realize that His Word, His promise of remembrance, is more substantial and dependable than any evidence of our senses. When He sends the visible evidence, that is well also; we appreciate it all the more after we have trusted Him without it. Those who are readiest to trust God without other evidence than His Word always receive the greatest number of visible evidences of His love.[81]—C. G. Trumbull

Relying on God has to begin all over again every day, as if nothing had yet been done.[82]—C. S. Lewis

"Yet the Lord will command his lovingkindness in the day time, and in the night his song shall be with me, and my prayer unto the God of my life.

"I will say unto God my rock, Why hast thou forgotten me? why go I mourning...?"

"Why art thou cast down, O my soul? and why art thou disquieted within me? hope thou in God: for I shall yet praise him, who is the health of my countenance, and my God."—Psalm 42:8–9, 11.

Part and parcel of life are storms that rock our boat, bringing hardship, fear and deep agony of soul. Life is difficult. But no part of life even comes close to the difficulty you presently are facing in the death of a loved one.

While I was a college student, a chapel speaker said something I have never forgotten, something I hope you will etch upon the walls of your mind. He simply said, "There's a tolerable solution for every intolerable problem you face." I have proved that statement to be true time and again. Life is hard, but God is good. He promises to walk

> Life is hard, but God is good. He promises to walk through every storm, sorrow, bitter disappointment, lonely moment, and failure with you.

through every storm, sorrow, bitter disappointment, lonely moment, and failure with you. He can do anything but fail you. Therefore fear not that which happens to or around you or loved ones, relying upon Him who will not "fail thee nor forsake thee."

The days of emotional and physical upheaval will PASS. The darkness eventually must give way to the light. God promises to still the boisterous winds and waves beating upon the vessel of your life, saying, "Peace, be still." Don't panic. Wait on Him. Trust in Him. He has not forsaken you. Soon the raging sea will become as glass, and tranquility will reign again.

"Be strong and of a good courage, fear not, nor be afraid of them: for the LORD thy God, he it is that doth go with thee; he will not fail thee, nor forsake thee."— Deuteronomy 31:6.

The Apostle Paul admonishes believers to "Rejoice in the Lord alway: and again I say, Rejoice" (Philippians 4:4). How is the believer to obey this command while in the midst of heavy sorrow? Is it feasible to believe that the Christian while under the burden of heavy grief can actually exhibit a heart attitude of joy?

John MacArthur provides this perspective on joy amidst sorrow: "Now it should be obvious that the command to rejoice is not then dependent upon positive circumstances...There is no event or circumstance that can occur in the life of any Christian that should diminish that Christian's joy. We are called to this incessant joy. It is a command, and the emphasis is on the unceasing aspect of this joy. Even when we suffer, Peter says in 1 Peter 4:13, we are to rejoice with joy, compounding the expression to remind us that this is not some minimal joy; this is not some marginal joy; but this is an incessant kind of joy that gathers up all of our being in its expression....

"Paul gives testimony there that he obeyed this command as a way of life. Even when he was sorrowing, sorrowing with the sorrow of others, sorrowing over the failure of believers in churches, sorrowing over the disaffection of those he loved, sorrowing over the pain of persecution, sorrowing more often than not over the maltreatment that the gospel preachers received, sorrowing over the dishonor that was literally placed upon Christ—and yet all of those kinds of emotional experiences never touched his joy. So in 2 Corinthians 6:10 does he say, 'As sorrowful yet always rejoicing.'...

"When we're told again to rejoice in the Lord always and again I will say rejoice, when it's reiterated, we bow the knee again and say, 'That's exactly right'; and we have the resource to do that. And the key, of course, is to look away from the changing circumstance to the unchangeable God, Christ, the Holy Spirit, the unchangeable benefits and blessings of our salvation, and the unchangeable promise of eternal Heaven so that the joyful Christian thinks more of his Lord than his personal difficulties, more of his spiritual riches in Christ than his poverty on earth, and more of his glorious fulfillment in Heaven than his present pain. Therein lies our joy.[83]

The Christian who maintains intimate fellowship with the Lord knows inner heart joy and peace despite suffering and pain. His joy relies not upon outward circumstances but a relationship with Jesus Christ.

13 What Loved Ones Are Doing in Heaven

"Christ comforts in bereavement by showing us what that which we call death really is to the Christian. If we could see what it is that happens to our beloved one when he leaves us—we could not weep!"[84]—J. R. Miller

R. G. Lee commented, "Heaven is the most marvelous place the wisdom of God could conceive and that the power of God could prepare."[85]

Someone observed, "What makes Heaven Heaven is God." If the streets were dirt instead of gold, if the walls were sheetrock instead of jasper, if the houses were more like huts than a Ritz-Carlton, it would still be Heaven because God is there. I don't know about you, but that's enough for me! Your loved one is in the presence of God. Wow!

A wondrous tale about a boy whose young sister was dying illustrates that which awaits the saint in death. The boy understood that if he could obtain a single leaf from the tree of life in the garden of God, she could be healed. He found the garden and implored the angel sentinel to give him one leaf. The angel consented to do so if he could promise that his sister would never again become sick, be unhappy, do wrong, be cold or hungry, or be treated harshly.

The boy was unable to make such a promise. The angel then opened the gate slightly, bidding the child look upon beauty of the garden. "Then, if you still wish it," said the angel, "I will myself ask the King for a leaf from the tree of life to heal your sister."

After looking upon the wondrous beauty within the gates of Heaven, the boy softly said, "I will not ask for the leaf now. There is no place in this entire world as beautiful as that. There is no friend as kind as the Angel of Death. I wish he would take me too!"[86]

> The Bible reveals in part not only what Heaven is like but what believers are doing in that glorious abode.

If only you could do as this young boy—look within the gate through which your loved one passed upon leaving you— comfort would fill your heart. And you *may* look, to limited degree, through the window of Holy Scripture. The Bible reveals in part not only what Heaven is like but what believers are doing in that glorious abode.

Saints serve God day and night (Revelation 7:15). Your loved one is busy with the ministry assignment given by God. "There'll be no idleness in Heaven. We will serve Him with perfect joy and happiness."[87] This service implies judging and ruling the world and the angels with God (Luke 19:17–19; 1 Corinthians 6:2–3).

W. A. Criswell stated, "We shall not be passive spectators, just observing; but we shall be an active, vital part of the whole re-created kingdom of God. We each shall have a service to render according to how God has made us and endowed us. As we differ in tastes, likes, looks, choices, and abilities, so also we shall differ in our separate assignments and activities."[88]

Saints sing in Heaven (Revelation 5:9). Saved loved ones are in the celestial choir forever singing, "Worthy is the Lamb that was slain to receive power, and riches, and wisdom, and strength, and honour, and glory, and blessing" (Revelation 5:12), and other praise songs in unceasing worship of God. Without doubt, your loved one has already joined George Bev Shea in singing *Victory in Jesus*.

Saints rest in Heaven (Revelation 14:13). Your loved one grew tired and worn, perhaps with battling sickness, the demands of livelihood, Christian ministry, and/or the foes of darkness. But "a day of rest" (Hebrews 4:9) is now their lot. Heaven is the "land of rest" the songwriter sighs for where he will lay his armor down and study war no more. Your loved one is presently in this land of rest.

Saints socialize in Heaven. "Jesus speaks of the shrewd servant's desire to use earthly resources so that 'people will welcome me into their houses.' Then Jesus tells his followers to use 'worldly wealth' (earthly resources) to 'gain friends' (by making a difference in their lives on earth), 'so that when it is gone [when life on earth is over], you will be welcomed into eternal dwellings' (Luke 16:9). Our 'friends' in Heaven appear to be those whom we've touched in a significant way on earth. They will apparently have their own 'eternal dwellings.' Luke 16:9 suggests these eternal dwelling places of friends could be places to fellowship and stay in as we move about the heavenly kingdom."[89] Your loved ones are enjoying the fellowship of friends and family who preceded them to Heaven.

Though all this is glorious, it fails to touch the hem of the garment as to all that loved ones do and experience in Heaven.

"No eye has seen, no ear has heard, and no mind has imagined what God has prepared for those who love him."—1 Corinthians 2:9 NLT.

But such as is known brings comfort.

Jeremy Camp reminds us of a day better than you face today:

There will be a day with no more tears,
No more pain, and no more fears.
There will be a day when the burdens of this place
Will be no more; we'll see Jesus face to face.[90]

Top Twelve Ways to Deal with Grief

"Grieving properly," comments J. I. Packer, "leads back to thinking properly, living properly, and praising properly. God sees to that! 'Blessed are those who mourn, for they will be comforted' (Matt. 5:4)."[91]

How might you handle the grief? How can you live with the grief in a way that is healthy for you and others and also honors God?

1. Talk about it to God and others (venting is healthy).

2. Absorb Holy Scripture through meditation and memorization (focus upon texts that speak of God's promises to comfort and help).

3. Engage in personal and corporate worship of God (adoration, exaltation, supplication, thanksgiving, and confession).

4. Interact with others, drawing support (avoid the "Job" type friends, see Chapter 14).

5. Resume responsibilities (decision making, work, school, church).

6. Get back to your familiar routine as much as possible and as soon as possible.

7. Spend time alone in God's presence (solitude).

8. Write about it (journaling).

9. Rest sufficiently to cope with grief properly.

10. Avoid isolation (not solitude).

11. Grab hold of God; gaze upon God; glorify God (overrule emotions that protest).

12. Prepare for grief triggers by having a plan in place that will lessen their impact.

14 Helpful or Hurtful Friends

"Can I see another's woe, And not be in sorrow too? Can I see another's grief, And not seek for kind relief?"[92]—William Blake

When three of Job's friends heard of the tragedy he had suffered, they got together and traveled from their homes to comfort and console him (Job 2:11).

Job's friends tried to help console him. When they heard of the tragedy, they immediately got together no doubt to pray for him and talk of how they might help him. Next they dropped everything at a moment's notice to travel a long distance to see him. Upon arrival, they didn't stay at the Ritz Carlton but sat with him on the ash heap. Their grief was so heavy for Job they could not speak for seven days. Despite all they did wrong, credit them for doing it with a caring, compassionate heart.

Job's friends certainly didn't help relieve his sorrow and pain; they only added to it. Sadly some well-meaning friends do the same with insensitive remarks, such as, "I know how you feel" (they don't; no one can); "It will take time, but you will get through this" (though true, it gives nothing for you to cling to now); "Everything will be okay" (but it's not okay; your heart is in a crucible of tremendous pain); "You must be strong for your children" (in reality, seeing how

73

you handle true grief is what they need most); "Everything works together for good" (truth for sure, but to someone whose eyes are blinded with tears of tremendous grief as yours are, perhaps not very comforting—at least presently); "It's been a month; aren't you over it yet?" (you will never be "over" it); and "At least you have two children left" (this is sort of like saying to a person who just lost one eye, "At least you have one eye left." The knowledge that he has one eye doesn't ease the pain of losing the other eye.)

> Probably the best things that can be shared to strengthen and comfort you are said without words.

Following the funeral service of his wife, Eugene Peterson and his twenty-year-old daughter sought isolation. As they sat together in silence weeping, a man interrupted. Peterson says, "He put his arm across my shoulder and spoke some preacherish clichés in a preacherish tone. Then, mercifully, he left. I said to my daughter, 'Karen, I hope I've never done that to anybody.'

"She said, 'Oh, Daddy, I don't think you have ever done that.' I hope not."[93]

Probably the best things that can be shared to strengthen and comfort you are said without words. You need friends to love on you, simply listen to you talk and cry (not dialogue), journey with you on the roller coaster of emotional sorrow that has its highs when God is felt near and dear and its possible lows of wondering if God has abandoned you. You need friends who will be your safe place to be yourself, to cry, talk, question, or doubt—without adding their two cents' worth unless asked.

Queen Victoria illustrates my point. Once she heard that the wife of a common laborer had lost her baby. Compassionately she called on the woman and spent some time with her. Neighbors afterwards made inquiry as to what the queen had said. "Nothing," replied the grieving mother. "She simply put her hands on mine, and we silently wept together."[94]

You need friends who primarily will reach out to you with a gentle, loving touch or a hug, who will allow their spirit and yours to communicate without the use of words. Charlie Walton in his book *When There Are No Words* explains the power of a hug in the hour of grief.

"Pain doesn't come in pounds or ounces or gallons. You just feel like you are standing before a mountain that you are going to have to move one spoonful at a time. It is a task you can never hope to complete...a mountain that you can never hope to finish moving.

"But...as you stand surveying that mountain of grief...a loved one steps forward with a hug that communicates clearly. You can almost picture that person stepping up to your mountain of grief with a shovel and saying, 'I cannot move the mountain for you...but I will take this one shovelful of your grief and deal with it myself.'"[95]

Walton continues, "Every hug helps to dilute the pain...to move the mountain. Don't be selfish with your mountain. Don't be a martyr about your grief. There is plenty of mountain to keep you busy the rest of your life...and...if your friends hadn't been willing to help...they wouldn't have showed up with those spoons, shovels and hugs."[96]

In the wilderness, a man became lost. He was approached by a man who met him, and the following conversation ensued. "Sir, I am lost. Can you show me the way out of this wilderness?"

"No," said the stranger, "I cannot show you the way out of the wilderness; but maybe if I walk with you, we can find it together."[97]

Though unable to tell us the way out of our sorrow, compassionate friends will walk with us until we find it.

15 Lessons from Other Grievers

You don't heal from the loss of a loved one because time passes you; you heal because of what you do with the time.[98] –Carol Crandall

"Bereavement is not the truncation of married love but one of its regular phases—like the honeymoon. What we want is to live our marriage well and faithfully through that phase, too."[99] These words of C. S. Lewis express the calling to husbands and wives after the other has died.

Though God and Holy Scripture are your stay in sorrow, help may be found from the experience of those who have been where you are now.

Though God and Holy Scripture are your stay in sorrow, help may be found from the experience of those who have been where you are now. The following statements are comprised of what grievers would say in general regarding coping with sorrow and loss.

Don't compare the grieving experience of others with your own. Don't fall into the trap of allowing the grieving experiences of others to dictate how you are to respond to grief. Each person is unique and will grieve differently. There will be things in common

77

with others who grieve, but not in the same sequence or time frame necessarily.

Stay close to God. Read the Bible, pray and worship. The psalmist David experienced many dark trials in life, including the death of his baby. The psalms tell of his brokenness in sorrow but also of how God sustained, supplying joy, hope and peace. Read the psalms and be ministered to by the Holy Spirit.

Get out. Call a friend for lunch, coffee or a walk. Return to church and its activities and ministries.

Recall the lifetime of memories shared with your loved one.

Moving forward, honor your loved one by fulfilling what he or she would want you to do. Accepting your loved ones' death is not forgetting them. You will never do that. Pressing forward is not saying you are over their death. That will never happen. Smiling and laughing is not demeaning to your loved ones. It is pleasing to them and to God. The Christian in death says, "Good night, see you in the morning," not, "Good-bye."

Get back to the routine of life—job, school or home.

Realize that others may finish their grieving before you do and think you should be over it also, causing them to resist speaking of your loved one.

Watch and prepare for "grief triggers," such as Christmas, Thanksgiving, Easter, birthdays, and the anniversary of your loved one's death that will wallop you with sadness. I experience them with regard to my parents; all will with regard to their deceased loved ones. It is natural. It will be helpful to prepare for such "trigger" days by conversing with loved ones regarding their observance (where, how, when).

Immediately following the death of a loved one, you hit "autopilot" and automatically do what is necessary regarding notification of family, the visitation night, and funeral. But after the funeral, the exodus of friends from the home, and the cessation of phone calls and sympathy cards, the loss hits home; and horrendous pain occurs. Sadly, this happens when most people think you are doing well, expecting the soon return to a life of normalcy. Friends need to realize they are needed the most after the funeral.

"And devout men carried Stephen to his burial, and made great lamentation over him."—Acts 8:2.

Stephen, the first Christian martyr, was carried to the cemetery by fellow believers who engaged in great lamentation [*kopetos*] over him. *Kopetos* refers to grief that is immeasurable. Note, not only did they engage in *kopetos* but "great" *kopetos* for him.

Friends who engage in "great" *kopetos* for you and your departed loved one are genuine, the real deal, and will be a source of great comfort if you will allow them to be.

Horatio Spafford and his family decided to join the D. L. Moody team on an evangelistic crusade in

79

Europe. Spafford's wife and four daughters departed without him; he was to join them in a week.

Tragically, the ship on which they were aboard collided with another vessel and sank within twenty minutes. Spafford's wife, Anna, was the only family survivor.

Ten days later from the hospital Anna sent her husband a message that consisted of two words: "Saved alone."

He was devastated and shook uncontrollably. Major Whittle, Spafford's friend, consoled him and traveled with him to France to see his wife.

En route, the captain awoke him at the spot where his children drowned, as he requested. Upon looking into the dark, cold water that now was their grave, he wept. He then sat down and penned the words of a hymn that has brought comfort and hope to many in their hour of grief.

When peace like a river attendeth my way,
When sorrows like sea billows roll,
Whatever my lot, Thou hast taught me to say,
"It is well, it is well with my soul."

Though Satan should buffet, though trials should
        come,
Let this blest assurance control,
That Christ has regarded my helpless estate
And hath shed His own blood for my soul.

And, Lord, haste the day when my faith shall be
      sight,
The clouds be rolled back as a scroll.
The trump shall resound, and the Lord shall
      descend—
Even so, it is well with my soul.[100]

Horatio Spafford in his devastation trusted God with his loss and grief. The brokenhearted person that leans on Jesus for repose is the only one that can sincerely say, "It is well with my soul."

16 Getting over It Too Soon

Following the death of his wife, C. S. Lewis wrote:

"Getting over it so soon? But the words are ambiguous. To say the patient is getting over it after an operation for appendicitis is one thing; after he's had his leg off is quite another. After that operation either the wounded stump heals or the man dies. If it heals, the fierce, continuous pain will stop. Presently he'll get back his strength and be able to stump about on his wooden leg. He has 'got over it.' But he will probably have recurrent pains in the stump all his life, and perhaps pretty bad ones; and he will always be a one-legged man.

"There will be hardly any moment when he forgets it. Bathing, dressing, sitting down and getting up again, even lying in bed will all be different. His whole way of life will be changed. All sorts of pleasures and activities that he once took for granted will have to be simply written off—duties too.

> The death of a loved one is like an amputation of an arm or a leg which you will live without for the rest of your life.

"At present I am learning to get about on crutches. Perhaps I shall presently be given a wooden leg. But I shall never be a biped [two-footed] again."[101]

Lewis is correct; you will never get over it, much less get over it too soon. The death of a loved one is like an amputation of an arm or a leg which you will live without for the rest of your life.

Death is a paradox. Your loved one is always with you (mentally) but not with you (physically)—but one day will be forever with you (mentally/physically in Heaven). So when psychiatrists talk of the grieving time frame being eighteen months to two years, they are referring to the major sorrow cycle or process, not its completion.

C. H. Spurgeon offers great consolation to those who sorrow. "The good news is that, by God's grace, in time the sorrowing sadness will lessen more and more, giving way to sweet sadness. Though sorrow will never be completely erased, by God's promises and the testimonies of others who have walked the same path, it will evolve into a life of heightened peace, hope and joy.

"Sorrow is not a stage you get through, but rather a process you live with. To say, "God, my Father," to put myself right into His hand and feel that I am safe there, to look up to Him though it is with tears in my eyes and feel that He loves me, and then to put my head right on His chest as the prodigal son did and sob my griefs out there into my Father's heart—oh, this is the death of grief and the life of all comfort.

"Isn't Jehovah called the God of all comfort? You will find Him so, beloved. He has been our help in ages past; He is our hope for years to come. If He had not been my help, then my soul would have utterly perished in the day of its suffering and its heartache.

"Oh, I bear testimony for Him this day that you cannot go to God and pour out your heart before Him without finding a wonderful comfort. When your friend cannot wipe away your tears, when you yourself with your best reasoning powers and your most courageous efforts cannot overcome your grief, when your heart beats fast and seems as if it would burst with grief, then as God's child, you will pour out your heart before Him.

"God is a refuge for us. He is our fortress, our refuge and defense. We only have to go to Him, and we will find that even here on earth God will wipe away every tear from our eyes."[102]

17 The Medicine of Solitude

"Our language has wisely sensed the two sides of being alone. It has created the word *loneliness* to express the pain of being alone. And it has created the word *solitude* to express the glory of being alone."[103]—Paul Tillich

Lord, in the midst of this storm, it is raining so hard that I cannot see where I am going. I really am trying to find my way—Your way. I squint my eyes trying desperately to see, but the rain and fog prevents it.

When will the rain stop and the fog dissolve, that I may see You clearly? When will the thunder and lightning that strikes unexpectedly, disrupting joy and peace, end? When will the sun in all its radiant beauty break forth upon my heart? It seems never. But I know it will. I abide beneath the umbrella of Thy protective and comforting care until it does. Until then, grant me new grace to mourn without murmuring, facing each day's challenges and changes in a manner that pleases You, and a heart of unrelenting trust that acknowledges Your control.

> The practice of solitude is the withdrawal of oneself to a quiet and serene place in silence before the Lord.

The practice of

solitude is the withdrawal of oneself to a quiet and serene place in silence before the Lord. Solitude is "a life-giving practice that enriches our hearts with the powerful gifts of clarity, cleansing, and strength" (Warden). William Wordsworth remarked, "Solitude permits the mind to feel."[104]

You certainly will have times when you want to be alone, to withdraw from family and friends and reflect upon what has happened, turning to God for assurance, comfort and guidance. In the time of solitude, you will find restfulness, a second wind and more of a handle on the present and future. Don't confuse solitude with isolation.

The duration of solitude may be a few minutes to several hours or days. Jesus practiced the discipline of solitude (Luke 4:42), as did the prophet Elijah at Mount Horeb (1 Kings 19:11–13) and the Apostle Paul in Arabia (Galatians 1:17). The Lord instructs, "Be still, and know that I am God" (Psalm 46:10). David declared,

"Truly my soul silently waits for God; From Him comes my salvation.

"He only is my rock and my salvation; He is my defense; I shall not be greatly moved."

"My soul, wait silently for God alone, For my expectation is from Him."—Psalm 62:1–2, 5 NKJV.

Andrew Murray emphasized the importance of solitude.

"It is good that a man quietly wait." Take time to be separate from all friends and all duties, all cares and all joys; time to be still and quiet before God. Take time not only to secure stillness from man and the world but from self and its energy. Let the Word and prayer be very precious. But remember, even these may hinder the quiet waiting."[105]

A. W. Tozer comments on solitude:

"Stay in the secret place till the surrounding noises begin to fade out of your heart and a sense of God's presence envelops you....Listen for the inward Voice till you learn to recognize it....Learn to pray inwardly every moment....Call home your roving thoughts. Gaze on Christ with the eyes of your soul. Practice spiritual concentration."[106]

As you wait before the Lord, listen for His still small voice. It's easier to talk to God than listen, especially in the time of great distress; but determine to do it. He wants to speak to you words of reassurance, comfort, love, and encouragement. Say with the child Samuel, "Lord...speak; for thy servant heareth" (1 Samuel 3:10).

In my times of solitude, I find journaling beneficial, the recording of my feelings and impressions from God. Such journaling helps vent pent-up feelings and enables focus on the next step. Remember that what is written down is for your benefit, not for the eyes of others to view.

"Words that express your grief," John Woodhouse wrote, "will speak predominantly of the good that we have lost. That is why we are grieving. Such words are appropriate and should be understood for what they are, not criticized because they overlook weaknesses, flaws, and failures. Putting our grief into words helps us understand our sadness by helping us see its cause—the good we have lost—and thank God for the goodness, because it was His gift to us."[107]

18 Signs of Getting through Grief

Those who navigate little streams and shallow creeks know very little about the God of tempests; but those who "go down to the sea in ships, that do business in great waters; These see the works of the LORD, and his wonders in the deep." Among the huge Atlantic waves of bereavement, poverty, temptation, and reproach, we learn the power of Jehovah, because we feel the littleness of man.[108]—C. H. Spurgeon

"While I will never grow accustomed to life without Ruth, she would be the first to scold me if I didn't look for God's plan for the here and now."[109]—Billy Graham

"Surely you know. Surely you have heard. The LORD is the God who lives forever, who created all the world. He does not become tired or need to rest. No one can understand how great his wisdom is.

"He gives strength to those who are tired and more power to those who are weak.

"Even children become tired and need to rest, and young people trip and fall.

"But the people who trust the LORD will become strong again. They will rise up as an eagle in the sky; they will run and not need rest; they will walk and not become tired."—Isaiah 40:28–31 NCV.

You know you're getting better in handling grief and moving in the right direction of overcoming it when the following things start to happen.[110]

You have an awareness of the fact your loved one is forever gone not to return.

Patterns of sleep, exercise and eating are returning to how they were prior to your loved one's death.

Time passes more frequently without dwelling on thoughts of your loved one (you will never forget them).

A new routine without your loved one is progressing. The many holes created by the absence of your loved one are now being filled by yourself and others (not all can/will be filled) with greater ease.

Entertainment (music, TV shows, sports, etc.) which you both enjoyed together, although painful at the first, now is becoming comfortable.

Things as they are in reality are accepted without trying to back up the hands of time to return to how it used to be.

The ability to laugh and engage in fun activities without feeling guilty returns.

You are able to stop a ritual like visiting the cemetery daily or weekly.

You take comfort in helping others who grieve.

Your reason to live is more and more evident.

19 Strength in Scripture

In the midst of the awesomeness, a touch comes, and you know it is the right hand of Jesus Christ. You know it is not the hand of restraint, correction, nor chastisement, but the right hand of the Everlasting Father. Whenever His hand is laid upon you, it gives inexpressible peace and comfort and the sense that "underneath are the everlasting arms," (Deuteronomy 33:27) full of support, provision, comfort, and strength.[111]—Oswald Chambers

In the Catacombs of Rome where Christians hid in times of persecution, one symbol is found written upon the walls more than any other—that of an anchor.[112] Believers have always found strength and comfort in life's storms knowing that they have an Anchor that holds them safe and secure. The Anchor is the sure promises of God recorded in the Holy Scripture.

"So God has given both his promise and his oath. These two things are unchangeable because it is impossible for God to lie. Therefore, we who have fled to him for refuge can have great confidence as we hold to the hope that lies before us.

"This hope is a strong and trustworthy anchor for our souls."—Hebrews 6:18–19 NLT.

The text is an analogy of olden days when most ships had sails. When such a ship approached a harbor difficult to navigate, the captain would send a seaman ahead in a small boat with the anchor attached to a rope that extended back to the ship. Once in the bay the seaman would drop the anchor. The captain then would give orders to the crew to pull the rope little by little, drawing the ship safely into the harbor. In the Christian life, Christ has gone before us to drop the anchor within the harbor of Heaven.[113]

Hold fast to the Anchor's rope, for it is the griever's indispensable source of strength and comfort and prevents you from drifting off course, ever drawing you Heavenward.

The Anchor is Scripture, God's promises, all of which ensure security, strength and stability amidst life's storms until life's journey ends in the harbor of the Celestial City.

Hold fast to the Anchor's rope, for it is the griever's indispensable source of strength and comfort and prevents you from drifting off course, ever drawing you Heavenward. Mediate upon and claim continuously the promises of Jesus which He spoke to troubled, broken hearts such as yours.

Regarding His promises, the famous evangelist D. L. Moody stated, "When a man says, 'I will,' it may not mean much. We very often say 'I will' when we don't mean to fulfill what we say. But when we come to the 'I will' of Christ, He means to fulfill it. Everything He promised to do, He is able and willing to accomplish. I cannot find any Scripture where He says 'I will' do this or 'I will' do that but that it will be done."[114]

"The LORD is close to the brokenhearted; he rescues those whose spirits are crushed."—Psalm 34:18 NLT.

"These things I have spoken unto you, that in me ye might have peace. In the world ye shall have tribulation: but be of good cheer; I have overcome the world."—John 16:33.

"I will turn their mourning into gladness; I will give them comfort and joy instead of sorrow."—Jeremiah 31:13.

"No, I will not abandon you or leave you as orphans in the storm—I will come to you."—John 14:18 TLB.

"I am leaving you with a gift—peace of mind and heart. And the peace I give is a gift the world cannot give. So don't be troubled or afraid."—John 14:27 NLT.

"What a wonderful God we have—he is the Father of our Lord Jesus Christ, the source of every mercy,

"And the one who so wonderfully comforts and strengthens us in our hardships and trials."—2 Corinthians 1:3–4 NLT.

"The LORD said, 'I have seen the misery of my people in Egypt, and I have heard them crying out because of the slave drivers. I know how much they're suffering.'"—Exodus 3:7 GWT.

"God is our refuge and strength, a very present help in trouble."—Psalm 46:1.

"He says, 'Don't be afraid, because I have saved you. I have called you by name, and you are mine.

"When you pass through the waters, I will be with you. When you cross rivers, you will not drown. When you walk through fire, you will not be burned, nor will the flames hurt you.

"This is because I, the LORD, am your God, the Holy One of Israel, your Savior....

"Because you are precious to me, because I give you honor and love you,...

"Don't be afraid, because I am with you.'"—Isaiah 43:1–5 NCV.

"Let not your heart be troubled: ye believe in God, believe also in me.

"In my Father's house are many mansions: if it were not so, I would have told you. I go to prepare a place for you.

"And if I go and prepare a place for you, I will come again, and receive you unto myself; that where I am, there ye may be also."—John 14:1–3.

Pray the following Scripture prayers unto God in response to His promise to console and give new grace for the hour of sorrow.

"O Lord, have mercy on me in my anguish. My eyes are red from weeping; my health is broken from sorrow."—Psalm 31:9 TLB.

"Turn to me and be gracious to me, for I am lonely and afflicted.

"Relieve the troubles of my heart and free me from my anguish.

"Look on my affliction and my distress and take away all my sins (Psalm 25:16—18 NIV).

"My God, my God, why have you abandoned me? Why are you so far away when I groan for help?

"Every day I call to you, my God, but you do not answer. Every night you hear my voice, but I find no relief.

"Yet you are holy, enthroned on the praises of Israel.

"Our ancestors trusted in you, and you rescued them.

"They cried out to you and were saved. They trusted in you and were never disgraced."—Psalm 22:1–5 NLT.

"Hear my prayer, O LORD, and let my cry come unto thee.

"Hide not thy face from me in the day when I am in trouble; incline thine ear unto me: in the day when I call answer me speedily.

"For my days are consumed like smoke, and my bones are burned as an hearth.

"My heart is smitten, and withered like grass; so that I forget to eat my bread."—Psalm 102:1–4.

"Hear me, Lord, and answer me, for I am poor and needy.

"Guard my life, for I am faithful to you; save your servant who trusts in you.

"You are my God; have mercy on me, Lord, for I call to you all day long.

"Bring joy to your servant, Lord, for I put my trust in you.

"You, Lord, are forgiving and good, abounding in love to all who call to you.

"Hear my prayer, Lord; listen to my cry for mercy.

"When I am in distress, I call to you, because you answer me.

"Among the gods there is none like you, Lord; no deeds can compare with yours.

"All the nations you have made will come and worship before you, Lord; they will bring glory to your name.

"For you are great and do marvelous deeds; you alone are God.

"Teach me your way, Lord, that I may rely on your faithfulness; give me an undivided heart, that I may fear your name.

"I will praise you, Lord my God, with all my heart; I will glorify your name forever.

"For great is your love toward me; you have delivered me from the depths, from the realm of the dead."—Psalm 86:1–13 NIV.

"Even when I go through the darkest valley, I fear no danger, for You are with me; Your rod and Your staff—they comfort me."—Psalm 23:4 HCSB.

20 When Answers Aren't Enough

"None spake a word unto him: for they saw that his grief was very great."—Job 2:13.

Grief is itself a medicine.[115]—William Cowper

We must learn to live on the heavenly side and look at things from above. To contemplate all things as God sees them, as Christ beholds them, overcomes sin, defies Satan, dissolves perplexities, lifts us above trials, separates us from the world, and conquers fear of death.[116]—A.B. Simpson

When you and I hurt deeply, what we really need is not an explanation from God but a revelation of God. We need to see how great God is; we need to recover our lost perspective on life. Things get out of proportion when we are suffering, and it takes a vision of something bigger than ourselves to get life's dimensions adjusted again.[117]—Warren Wiersbe

Theologians have a term for this: *Deus Absconditus*—the God who is hidden. This is when no light is thrown on the "why" of your suffering. This is when the usual means of grace—prayer, worship, singing, God's word—have no effect on the drooping spirit; when the tried and true formulas from books and seminars sound hollow; when you discover there are some things you cannot praise or pray your way out of...When God withdraws the light, He is trying to teach us that there is something better than light—faith.[118]—Ron Dunn

Whatever answers the doctor, friends, family, or perhaps even your minister gives for the death of your loved one may simply not satisfy or ease the hurt. They may never. In truth, no answer is sufficient to salve your broken heart. Scott Wesley Brown reminds us that

When answers aren't enough, there is Jesus.
He is more than just an answer to your prayer,
And your heart will find a safe and peaceful refuge.
When answers aren't enough, He is there.[119]

He is the "Hub" of the wheel of your life, the One who sustains, guides, provides and strengthens—"Christ, who is our life" (Colossians 3:4).

In facing this crisis, it's important to make Jesus central, not questions or answers or friends or even family. He is the "Hub" of the wheel of your life, the One who sustains, guides, provides and strengthens—"Christ, who is our life" (Colossians 3:4). No one, absolutely no one cares for and grieves with you more than Jesus.

The great Physician now is near,
    The sympathizing Jesus;
He speaks the drooping heart to cheer.
    Oh! hear the voice of Jesus.[120]

    Charles F. Weigle attests the same truth in "No One Ever Cared for Me Like Jesus."

I would love to tell you what I think of Jesus,
    Since I found in Him a friend so strong and true.
I would tell you how He changed my life completely;
    He did something that no other friend could do.

No one ever cared for me like Jesus;
    There's no other friend so kind as He.
No one else could take the sin and darkness from
      me.
    Oh, how much He cared for me.[121]

    Robert Louis Stevenson tells the story of a ship that was caught in a terrific storm, threatening the lives of its passengers. Against orders, one passenger braved the storm to get to the pilot's house. He observed the steersman at his post steadily holding the wheel, turning it inch by inch and turning the ship back to sea. The pilot, seeing the passenger, smiled. The daring passenger, upon returning below deck where others awaited, said cheerfully, "I have seen the face of the pilot, and he smiled. All is well."[122]

Amidst the voracious storms of sorrow pounding the ship of your life, its Pilot is smiling, giving assurance all will be well.

Family, friends and even the church may be spokes in the "wheel" that encourage, console, and spur you onward; but never cease to remember that Jesus is the "Hub" that moves and sustains your life. "Christ, who is our life" (Colossians 3:4)—He can do anything but fail or forsake you.

"To put everything in one," states C. H. Spurgeon, "there is nothing you can want; there is nothing you can ask for; there is nothing you can need in time or in eternity; there is nothing living, nothing dying; there is nothing in this world, nothing in the next world; there is nothing now, nothing at the resurrection morning, nothing in Heaven which is not contained in this text: "I will never leave thee, nor forsake thee."[123]

Cling to Jesus and this His glorious promise, and find solace for your soul. Jesus has not abandoned you, despite what circumstances and emotions seem to say. In fact, He has never been closer. In times when you may not *feel* His presence, "faith" His presence; for He is there just the same. Such knowledge assures that everything is going to be okay.

21 A Lesson from Grieving Caterpillars

"You never get over grief completely until you express it fully."[124]—Chuck Swindoll

Cartoonist Arthur Brisbane pictured a crowd of grieving caterpillars carrying the corpse of a cocoon to its final resting place. The poor, distressed caterpillars, attired in black clothing, were weeping and greatly distraught at the death of their friend. But all the while their friend, now a beautiful butterfly, fluttered happily above them, totally free from its earthly shell. To the grieving caterpillars, his death was mysterious and saddening; but to him it was glorious, freeing and exhilarating.[125]

In the cartoon, Brisbane sought to convey the mistake so often made at funerals, focusing only on the cocoon and attention on the deceased body while forgetting the bright, beautiful butterfly. The Lord has the final word concerning death, and He says, "I am the resurrection, and the life: he that believeth in me, though he were dead, yet shall he live" (John 11:25).

"God will not turn away," says John Piper, "from doing you good. He will keep on doing good. He doesn't do good to His children sometimes and bad to them other times. He keeps on doing good, and He never will stop doing good for ten thousand ages of ages. When things are going bad, that does not mean God has stopped doing good. It means He is shifting things around to get them in place for more good, if you will go on loving Him."[126]

There will be a happy meeting in Heaven, I know,
When we see the many loved ones we've known
      here below,
Gathered on that blessed hilltop with hearts all aglow,
That will be a glad reunion day.[127]

"And now, dear brothers and sisters, we want you to know what will happen to the believers who have died so you will not grieve like people who have no hope.

"For since we believe that Jesus died and was raised to life again, we also believe that when Jesus returns, God will bring back with him the believers who have died.

"We tell you this directly from the Lord: We who are still living when the Lord returns will not meet him ahead of those who have died.

"For the Lord himself will come down from heaven with a commanding shout, with the voice of the archangel, and with the trumpet call of God. First, the Christians who have died will rise from their graves.

"Then, together with them, we who are still alive and remain on the earth will be caught up in the clouds to meet the Lord in the air. Then we will be with the Lord forever.

"So encourage each other with these words."
—1 Thessalonians 4:13–18 NLT.

22 Death Is a Comma, Not a Period

"Death is not a period but a comma in the story of life."—Amos J. Traver.

In English grammar, a period at the conclusion of a sentence means "the end; nothing more is coming; the thought has been completed." In contrast, a comma loudly states, "Take a breath; relax a moment. Get prepared, for there is more to come."

What a wonderful description of death! Death is not a period to one's life,

> Death is not a period to one's life, only a comma indicating "the best is yet to be."

only a comma indicating "the best is yet to be." When everything seems to cry out that death is the end to your loved one, remember when Jesus rose from the dead He forever made it a "comma."

"Jesus said unto her, I am the resurrection, and the life: he that believeth in me, though he were dead, yet shall he live."—John 11:25.

"You who believe in Christ," stated C. H. Spurgeon, "ought no more to dread death than you dread going to sleep at night. You will, ere you sleep, commit yourself to God; and as you put your head on the pillow, the similitude of death will be upon you, even sleep which one has called 'death's cousin.' You will not be afraid of that. Why, then, should any dismay seize you in prospect of that which is but another sleep?"[128]

A Bend in the Road

Sometimes we come to life's crossroads,
　　And we view what we think is the end.
But God has a much wider vision,
　　And he knows that it's only a bend.

The road will go on and get smoother,
　　And after we've stopped for a rest,
The path that lies hidden beyond us
　　Is often the path that is best.

So rest and relax and grow stronger;
　　Let go and let God share your load.
And have faith in a brighter tomorrow—
　　You've just come to a bend in the road.[129]

23 Prepare to See Your Loved One Again

Who is going to be crying at your funeral? These are the people you should be spending time with right now in your life.[130]—Patrick Morley

C. H. Spurgeon comments on life after death:

Living near the cross of Calvary, thou mayest think of death with pleasure and welcome it when it comes with intense delight. It is sweet to die in the Lord; it is a covenant blessing to sleep in Jesus. Death is no longer banishment; it is a return from exile, a going home to the many mansions where the loved ones already dwell. The distance between glorified spirits in Heaven and militant saints on earth seems great, but it is not so. We are not far from home—a moment will bring us there. The sail is spread; the soul is launched upon the deep. How long will be its voyage?...

Listen to the answer, 'Absent from the body, present with the Lord.' Yon ship has just departed, but it is already at its haven. It did but spread its sail, and it was there. Like that ship of old upon the Lake of Galilee—a storm had tossed it, but Jesus said, "Peace, be still"; and immediately it came to land. Think not that a long period intervenes between the instant of death and the eternity of glory. When the eyes close on earth, they open in heaven.[131]

Becoming a Christian (entering into a personal relationship with Jesus Christ) is necessary in order to go to Heaven to see Jesus and saved loved ones. To become a Christian involves three things.

Understand that God loves you and desires a personal relationship with you.

"For God so loved the world, that he gave his only begotten Son, that whosoever believeth in him should not perish, but have everlasting life."—John 3:16.

Understand that sin (disobedience to God) has hindered this personal relationship and must be removed so you may be reconciled (made right) with God.

Agree with God's diagnosis of your condition (separation from Him due to sin) and be willing to have it remedied. The Bible says,

"For all have sinned, and come short of the glory of God."—Romans 3:23.

"The wages of sin is death; but the gift of God is eternal life through Jesus Christ our Lord."—Romans 6:23.

Understand that Jesus Christ alone can cleanse the heart of sin, making you right with God.

Jesus Christ alone is man's Savior from his sins and Doorway to Heaven.

Nothing you have done or may do (not baptism, religious work, goodness, or church attendance) can make you right with God. Jesus Christ alone is man's Savior from his sins and Doorway to Heaven.

"For when we were yet without strength, in due time Christ died for the ungodly."—Romans 5:6.

"The blood of Jesus Christ his Son cleanseth us from all sin."—1 John 1:7.

"I am the way, the truth, and the life: no man cometh unto the Father, but by me."—John 14:6.

"For whosoever shall call upon the name of the Lord shall be saved."—Romans 10:13.

Jesus died upon the cross and was raised from the dead to make possible divine forgiveness. He alone reconciles [makes right] man with God, enabling a personal relationship instantly to take place.

"For there is one God, and one mediator between God and men, the man Christ Jesus;

"Who gave himself a ransom for all, to be testified in due time."—1 Timothy 2:4–5.

Act Now

My friend, will you at this moment receive God's gracious gift of forgiveness of sin and promise of

Heaven at death by inviting Christ Jesus into your life as Lord and Savior? Own up to acts of disobedience and rebellion toward God, asking His forgiveness with a sincere and repentant (change of mind) heart (Acts 20:21). Right now, pray, using your own words—or, if you prefer, the following prayer—and accept God's gracious invitation of eternal life. It is not the prayer that will save you but He who hears it.

"God, please have mercy on me, a sinner. I realize that while my sin is inexcusable, it is forgivable through the death, burial and resurrection of Your Son, Jesus Christ. Jesus, I invite you into my heart as Lord and Savior to reign as unrivaled King of kings and Lord of lords. I turn my back on yesterday to live anew for You. In Jesus' name I do pray. Amen."

The Savior is waiting to enter your heart;
   Why don't you let Him come in?
There's nothing in this world to keep you apart;
   What is your answer to Him?[132]

Get Personal Documents Together

In the event of your death, family members should not have to look in every crook and crevice in search of personal documents.

Gather up important documents, including funeral plans, life insurance policies, birth certificate, checking/savings accounts, Last Will and Testament, personal loans to others and user name/passwords to Internet accounts.

Examine the documents and passwords, discarding what no longer is valid.

Store the documents in a central place (bank deposit box, home safe, file cabinet, shoe box, etc.).

Make the location of these documents known to your loved ones, and make this location easily accessible to them.

Review the documents annually, making it a habit to update them upon your birthday each year, if necessary.

Endnotes

[1] Cushing, William O. "Under His Wings." http://www.ccesonline.com/hymns/hymns.htm, accessed April 5, 2013.

[2] Doudney, Sarah. "The Christian's Good-night." http://www.bartleby.com/294/594.html.

[3] à Kempis, Thomas. *The Imitation of Christ,* Book III: On Inward Consolation. (New York: P. F. Collier & Son Company, 1909–14; New York: Bartleby.com, 2001).

[4] http://www.greatest-inspirational-quotes.com/death-quotes.html, accessed April 8, 2013.

[5] Morgan, R. J. *Nelson's Complete Book of Stories, Illustrations, and Quotes* (electronic ed.). (Nashville: Thomas Nelson Publishers, 2000), 767.

[6] Spurgeon, C. H. *The Death of the Christian.* (The New Park Street Pulpit, September 9, 1855), http://www.spurgeon.org/sermons/0043.htm, accessed April 2, 2013.

[7] "What Death Means for the Believer in Christ." Bible.org, accessed January 2, 2006.

[8] Criswell, W. A. "Grief at the Death of Family/Friends." http://www.wacriswell.com, accessed April 3, 2013.

[9] Marshall, Catherine. *A Man Called Peter.* penn.betatesters.com/peter05.htm, accessed April 4, 2013.

[10] http://christian-quotes.ochristian.com/Death-Quotes, accessed March 26, 2013.

[11] "Hope after Death." sermons.logos.com/submissions/83682-Hope-after-death, accessed April 5, 2013.

[12] http://christian-quotes.ochristian.com/Death-Quotes, accessed March 26, 2013.

[13] Spurgeon, C. H. "Death—A Sleep." Metropolitan Tabernacle Pulpit (Sermon #3077), http://www.spurgeongems.org/vols52-54/chs3077.pdf, accessed May 10, 2013.

[14] http://christian-quotes.ochristian.com/Death-Quotes, accessed March 26, 2013.

[15] Graham, Franklin, and Donna Lee Toney. *Billy Graham in Quotes.* (Nashville: Thomas Nelson, 2011), 98.

[16] Packer, J. I. *Knowing God.* (Downers Grove, IL: InterVarsity Press, 1993), 41–42.

[17] Packer, J. I. *A Grief Sanctified.* (Ann Harbor, Michigan: Servant Publications, 1997), 189.

[18] Jensen, Gorden. www.namethathymn.com, accessed April 22, 2013.

Endnotes

[19] Lorenz, Edmund S. "Tell It to Jesus." http://cyberhymnal.org, accessed April 22, 2013.

[20] Meyer, F. B., C. H. Spurgeon, Albert Barnes, and Others. *Funeral Sermons and Outlines.* (Grand Rapids: Baker Book House, 1955), 44–45.

[21] Card, Michael. *A Sacred Sorrow.* (Colorado Springs, Colorado: NavPress, 2005), 11.

[22] Becker, Randy. *Everyday Comfort.* (Grand Rapids, Michigan: Baker Books, 2006), 63.

[23] MacArthur, John. "Dealing with Sorrow." April 5, 2004. http://www.gty.org/resources/daily-devotion/DN462/Dealing-with-Sorrow, accessed March 29, 2005.

[24] Criswell, W. A. "In Memoriam." www.wacriswell.com, accessed April 3, 2013.

[25] Rice, John R. *The Son of God.* (Murfreesboro, TN: Sword of the Lord Publishers, 1976), 233.

[26] Stevens, Marsha. lyrics.christiansunite.com, accessed April 19, 2013.

[27] Elliot, Elizabeth. *The Strange Ashes.* (Grand Rapids, Michigan: Revell, 2004), 151.

[28] Graham, Billy. "Joy in Sorrow," Billy Graham's Daily Devotion, October 19, 2013. www.billygraham.org, accessed April 6, 2013.

[29] Spurgeon, C. H. *The Treasury of David.* (Grand Rapids, Michigan: Kregel Publications, 2004), Psalm 30:5.

[30] Ziglar, Zig. *Confessions of a Grieving Christian.* (Nashville: B and H Books, 2004), 43.

[31] Swindoll, Chuck. "Expressing Grief." November 29, 2011. http://www.insight.org/library/insight-for-today/expressing-grief.html, accessed March 31, 2011.

[32] Cowman, L. B. *Streams in the Desert.* (Grand Rapids, Michigan: Zondervan, 1997), January 5 entry.

[33] Sweeting, George. *The Joys of Successful Aging.* (Chicago: Moody Publishers, 2008), 141.

[34] Wood, A. Skevington. "Not for Sale." *Lansdowne Magazine* (Bournemouth, England: The Bourne Press, Spring 1971), 8.

[35] Ibid.

[36] Criswell, W. A. "Grief at the Death of Family/Friends." http://www.wacriswell.com, accessed April 3, 2013.

[37] Havner, 12.

[38] Author unknown.

[39] Hyles, Jack. *Meet the Holy Spirit.* (Hammond, IN: Hyles-Anderson Publishers, 1982), Chapter 17

Endnotes

[40] Adams, Jay E. *Shepherding God's Flock.* (Grand Rapids, Michigan: Zondervan, 1974), 136.

[41] Hsu, Albert Y. *Grieving a Suicide: A Loved One's Search for Comfort, Answers and Hope.* (Downers Grove, Ill.: InterVarsity, 2002), 41.

[42] Dunn, Ronald. *When Heaven is Silent: Trusting God When Life Hurts.* (Nashville: Thomas Nelson Publishers, 1994).

[43] http://www.helpguide.org/mental/grief_loss.htm, assessed April 11, 2013.

[44] Yancy, Phillip. "Where Is God When It Hurts." http://www.christianitytoday.com/ct/2007/june/14.55.html?start=4, accessed April 14, 2013.

[45] Ziglar, Zig. *Confessions of a Grieving Christian.* (Nashville: B and H Books, 2004), 136.

[46] Card, Michael. *A Sacred Sorrow.* (Colorado Springs, Colorado: NavPress, 2005), 83.

[47] MacArthur, John. *Safe in the Arms of Jesus.* (Nashville: Thomas Nelson , 2003), 133–134.

[48] Criswell, W. A. "The Beginning and the End of Sorrows." www.wacriswell.com, accessed April 2, 2013.

[49] Graham, Billy. "God Always Helps Overcome Sorrow." *The Palm Beach Post*—May 2, 1967.

[50] wiki.answers.com. Who wrote, "Our Father is too wise to be mistaken; our Father is too good to be unkind, so when you can't see His plan, when you can't trace His hand, trust His heart?"

[51] Miller, J. R. "Afterward You Will Understand (1909). http://www.gracegems.org/Miller/afterward_you_will_underst and.htm, accessed August 15, 2013.

[52] Elliot, Elizabeth. http://www.goodreads.com/author/quotes/6264.Elisabeth_Elli ot?page=3, accessed April 1, 2013.

[53] Henry, Matthew. *Matthew Henry's Commentary on the Whole Bible,* John 14:2. (Peabody, MA: Hendrickson Publishers, 2008).

[54] Courson, Jon. *Jon Courson's Application Commentary.* (Nashville: Thomas Nelson, 2003), 555.

[55] Hutson, Curtis, Ed. *Great Preaching on Comfort.* (Murfreesboro, TN: Sword of the Lord Publishers, 1990), 164–165.

[56] Hutson, Curtis, Ed. *Great Preaching on Heaven.* (Murfreesboro, TN: Sword of the Lord Publishers, 1987), 15.

[57] MacArthur, John. "The Solution to a Troubled Heart." http://www.gty.org, accessed May 22, 2013.

Endnotes

[58] Longfellow, Henry Wadsworth. www.goodreads.com, accessed April 6, 2013.

[59] Criswell, W. A., and Paige Patterson. *Heaven.* (Carol Stream, IL: Tyndale House Publishers), 34.

[60] Ibid., 42.

[61] Geisler, Norman. "The Significance of Christ's Physical Resurrection," in *Bibliotheca Sacra,* 146 (April–June 1989), 150.

[62] www.johnankerberg.org, "Evidence for the Resurrection of Christ from the Dead," accessed April 18, 2013.

[63] Cowman, C. "Consolation," p. 70. Bible.org, accessed April 6, 2013.

[64] Brumley, Albert E. "I Will Meet You in the Morning." http://hymnal.calvarybaptistsv.org/84.htm, accessed April 22, 2013.

[65] dailychristianquote.com/dcqredpath.html, accessed March 29, 2013.

[66] Graeff, Frank E. "Does Jesus Care?," 1901. Public domain. http://library.timelesstruths.org/music/Does_Jesus_Care/accessed March 27, 2013.

[67] Lockyer, Herbert. "The Death of the Saints," *The Sword of the Lord.* (Murfreesboro, TN: Sword of the Lord Publishers, March 29, 2013), 11.

[68] Ibid.

[69] Lewis, C. S. *A Grief Observed.* (New York: HarperOne, 2001), 15.

[70] Packer, J. I. *A Grief Sanctified.* (Ann Harbor, Michigan: Servant Publications, 1997), 12.

[71] Spurgeon, C. H. "Contentment," A Sermon (No. 320). Delivered on Sabbath Evening, March 25, 1860, New Park Street Chapel. www.spurgeon.org/sermons/0320.htm, accessed May 3, 2013. Bracketed comment is that of the author.

[72] Rogers, Adrian. "Dealing with Depression." http://www.sermonsearch.com, assessed April 11, 2013.

[73] http://christian-quotes.ochristian.com/Depression-Quotes, assessed April 11, 2013.

[74] Havner, 27.

[75] http://dailychristianquote.com/dcqlonely.html, accessed April 20, 2013.

[76] Morris, Henry M. *The Defender's Study Bible.* (Nashville: Thomas Nelson, 1995 edition), 1154.

[77] Havner, 10.

[78] Faulk, Timothy. Personal communication, April 10, 2013.

Endnotes

[79] Stork, Theophilus. *Sermons.* (Philadelphia: Lutheran Publication Society, 1876), 213.

[80] Crosby, Fanny. "Safe in the Arms of Jesus." http://cyberhymnal.org, accessed April 16, 2013.

[81] Cowman, L. B. *Streams in the Desert.* (Grand Rapids, Michigan: Zondervan, 1997), February 27.

[82] Martindale, Wayne, and Jerry Root, Editors. *The Quotable Lewis.* (Grand Rapids: Tyndale House, 1989), 156.

[83] MacArthur, John. "Rejoice Always." http://www.gty.org/resources/Sermons/80-266, accessed April 12, 2013

[84] Miller, J. R. "The Beatitude of Sorrow," (1891). http://www.gracegems.org/Miller/beatitude_for_sorrow.htm, accessed March 28, 2013.

[85] thecallforward.wordpress.com, accessed April 17, 2013.

[86] Ibid.

[87] Ford, Herschel. *Simple Sermons on Heaven, Hell, and Judgment.* (Grand Rapids: Zondervan, 1969), 26.

[88] Criswell, W. A., and Paige Patterson. *Heaven* (Carol Stream, IL: Tyndale House Publishers), 33.

---

89 Alcorn, Randy. "Questions and Answers about Heaven." www.precious-testimonies.com/Exhortations/f-j/heaven.htm, accessed April 21, 2011.

90 Camp, Jeremy. "There Will Be a Day." http://www.azlyrics.com, accessed April 4, 2013.

91 Packer, J. I. *A Grief Sanctified.* (Ann Harbor, Michigan: Servant Publications, 1997), 189–190.

92 Blake, William. "On Another's Sorrow." thinkexist.com/quotation/can_i_see_another-s.../150005.html. accessed March 30, 2013.

93 Card, Michael. *A Sacred Sorrow.* (Colorado Springs, Colorado: NavPress, 2005), 12.

94 Source unknown.

95 Walton, Charlie. *When There Are No Words.* (Ventura, CA: Pathfinder Publishing, 1999), 50–51.

96 Ibid., 51.

97 Nester, Emery. http://www.crazyforcody.com/favorite-inspirations.html, accessed March 31, 2013.

98 Staudacher, Carol. *A Time to Grieve.* (New York: HarperCollins Publishers, 1994), 92.

Endnotes

[99] Lewis, C. S. *A Grief Observed.* (New York: HarperOne, 2001), Foreword.

[100] Spafford, Horatio. "It Is Well with My Soul." http://www.hymnsite.com, accessed April 19, 2013.

[101] Lewis, C. S. *A Grief Observed.* (New York: HarperOne, 2001), 65–66.

[102] Spurgeon, C. H. "No Tears in Heaven." August 6, 1865. http://www.biblebb.com, accessed April 1, 2013.

[103] "Grief Healing." http://www.griefhealingblog.com/2012/02/loneliness-and-solitude-in-grief.html, accessed March 29, 2013.

[104] Wordsworth, 508 (Christian Basics 101 book)

[105] Murray, Waiting, 108–109 (Christian basics book)

[106] Wiersbe, Warren W. *Best of Tozer,* 151–152 (Christian basics book)

[107] *Moore Matters*, a publication of Moore College, (Newtown, NSW., Autumn, 2011), 13.

[108] Spurgeon, C. H. "Direction in Dilemma." A Sermon Delivered on Sunday Morning, November 22, 1863, at The Metropolitan Tabernacle, Newington. www.answersingenesis.org/articles/2010/07/16/direction-in-dilemma, March 30, 2013.

[109] "Billy Graham Offers Advice on Growing Old." March 5, 2013. http://blog.christianitytoday.com/ctliveblog/archives/2013/03/billy-graham-offers-advice-on-growing-old.html, accessed April 21, 2013.

[110] Fitzgerald, Helen. "Grief Recovery: You Know You're Getting Better When...." legacy.com, accessed April 1, 2013. Adapted.

[111] Chambers, Oswald. *My Utmost for His Highest*. (Grand Rapids, Michigan: Discovery House Publishers; Updated edition, 1992), May 24 entry.

[112] Courson, Jon. *Jon Courson's Application Commentary*. (Nashville: Thomas Nelson, 2003), 1472.

[113] Blackwood, Andrew W. *The Funeral*. (Grand Rapids: Baker Book House, 1942), 140.

[114] Moody, D. L. *The Seven 'I Will's' of Christ*. www.jesus-is-savior.com/Books, accessed May 22, 2013.

[115] www.wisdomquotes.com/quote/william-cowper.htm, accessed April 5, 2013.

[116] http://christian-quotes.ochristian.com, accessed April 21, 2013.

[117] Wiersbe, Warren W. *Why Us? When Bad Things Happen to God's People*. (Grand Rapids: Fleming H. Revell, 1984)

[118] Dunn, Ronald. *When Heaven Is Silent: Trusting God When Life Hurts.* (Nashville: Thomas Nelson Publishers, 1994).

[119] Brown, Scott Wesley. "When Answers Are Not Enough, There Is Jesus." www.bensonsound.com/lyrics/1095.htm, accessed March 30, 2013.

[120] Hunter, William. "The Sympathizing Jesus." http://www.cyberhymnal.org/htm/g/r/greatphy.htm, accessed March 30, 2013.

[121] Weigle, Charles F. "No One Ever Cared for Me Like Jesus." Hymnary.org, accessed March 30, 2013.

[122] sermonillustrations.com, accessed April 7, 2013.

[123] Spurgeon, C. H. *Morning and Evening,* February 23 (Morning). (Peabody, MA: Hendrickson Publishers, 1990).

[124] Swindoll, Chuck. "Expressing Grief," November 29, 2011. http://www.insight.org/library/insight-for-today/expressing-grief.html, accessed March 31, 2011.

[125] sermons.logos.com/submissions/102878-Illustrations. Accessed March 30, 2013.

[126] Piper, John. *The Pleasures of God: Meditations on God's Delight in Being God.* (Colorado Springs: Multnomah Books, 2000), 181.

[127] Pace, Adger M. http://www.hymnary.org, accessed April 22, 2013.

[128] Spurgeon, C. H. "His Own Funeral Sermon" (Metropolitan Tabernacle Pulpit, Sermon No. 2243), http://www.spurgeon.org/sermons/2243.htm, accessed April 6, 2013.

[129] Rice, Helen Steiner. bgmcclure.com/Archives/Bend2.htm, accessed March 30, 2013.

[130] www.sermonsearch.com, accessed April 3, 2013.

[131] Spurgeon, C. H. *Morning and Evening,* April 20 (Morning). (Peabody, MA: Hendrickson Publishers, 1990).

[132] Carmichael, Ralph. "The Savior Is Waiting to Enter Your Heart." http://www.angelfire.com/nf/music4christ/t-z/thesaviorislyrics.html, accessed April 1, 2013.

CPSIA information can be obtained
at www.ICGtesting.com
Printed in the USA
FFOW02n1505240116
20719FF